fun family festivals

Nanette Goings

Dedication

"From the rising of the sun to the place where it sets,
the name of the Lord is to be praised" (Psalm 113:3).

This book for families is dedicated to my family. To Bob, my patient husband and computer whiz, and to Mollie and Seth, my expert field-testers.

Fun Family Festivals

©1999 Nanette Goings

Published by The Standard Publishing Company, Cincinnati, Ohio 45231. A division of Standex International Corporation.

Credits
Produced by Susan L. Lingo, Bright Ideas Books™
Illustrated by Stacey Lamb
Cover design by Liz Howe
Cover illustration by Stacey Lamb

06 05 04 03 02 01 00 99   5 4 3 2 1
ISBN 0-7847-0910-6
Printed in the United States of America

Contents

LET'S CELEBRATE!

Finally, a family-centered book of super celebrations, happening hooplas, and frolicking festivals that are sure to become favorites with your church families! Whether traditional or totally unique, families will share serious festival fun as they learn serious God-centered truths and biblical lessons. Here's what *Fun Family Festivals* offers you and the families in your church:

★ **Family-centered fun with Bible-bound learning!** These aren't frivolous festivities but celebrations of the love, life, and laughter God has given us. Are there any better reasons to celebrate? And each family fête is centered around a memorable Bible story and a meaningful Scripture verse that is read and discussed by families.

★ **Simple set-up, simple supplies!** You choose which activities are suited to your group, then purchase just the supplies needed for those activities. Why, there's even a festival shopping list on the next page for you to photocopy and use. What could be easier?

★ **An intergenerational family approach!** Whether you define a family as a mom and dad with children, a single parent with an only child, a couple with grown children, grandparents, or simply a single member of the larger church family, you can invite everyone to come and celebrate as part of God's family! The festivals included in *Fun Family Festivals* are all-inclusive—just as God intended his love to be!

★ **Family fusion—to God and to each other!** People will feel frisky and light-hearted as they share fun, cooperation, and communication with other family members. Plus, the more serious family prayer time gives each family an opportunity to approach God as one, close-knit family unit joined in his love. What a gift to offer the families in your church!

So toss the confetti, inflate the balloons, and start addressing those invitations to fun as you joyfully leap into some of the best times your church family will ever remember!

LET'S PLAN A PARTY!

FESTIVAL TITLE:

_____

Date:
_____

Time:
_____

DECORATIONS AND INVITATIONS:

- _____   - _____
- _____   - _____
- _____   - _____

FESTIVAL GAMES

Game 1: _____   Game 2: _____

- _____   - _____
- _____   - _____
- _____   - _____

FESTIVAL CRAFTS

Craft 1: _____   Craft 2: _____

- _____   - _____
- _____   - _____
- _____   - _____

FESTIVAL FOOD

- _____   - _____
- _____   - _____
- _____   - _____

FESTIVAL FINALE

- _____   - _____
- _____   - _____

BRING THE FAMILY!

CELEBRATE WITH US AT THE

_____

When:

_____

Where:

_____

Time:

_____

FAMILY FUN!

GAMES!

FOOD!

CRAFTS & MORE!

Family Faith Builder:

Hope

LET'S BEGIN BREAKFAST

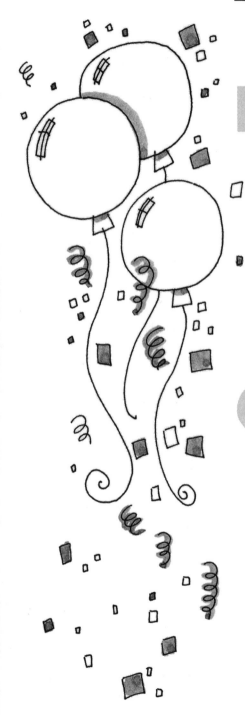

Start the new year focused on new beginnings.

BIBLE BASIS: 2 Thessalonians 2:15-17

With each new year comes renewed hope for fresh beginnings in our lives. Some may take up new hobbies or start new exercise programs. Many of us make resolutions for life changes we hope to accomplish in the coming year. What hope and joy Christians feel in knowing that God is the God of second chances and new beginnings! Share this special celebration breakfast with your church family—and revel in the sense of hope that God offers with the promise of each new year and the dawning of every new day!

GETTING READY

Each activity in this family festival contains its own list of simple supplies. Simply choose and use the activities that fit your needs and time requirements, then gather the appropriate supplies. Use one or more of these decorating and invitation suggestions to enliven your special event:

★ Make construction-paper invitations to look like sunny-side up eggs. Include the time and location of your event, as well as a note for each family to bring one pint-sized jar and lid. The jars will be used in one of the festival craft ideas. Make eight extra paper eggs to use in the Eggs-Over-Easy Relay.

★ Get early morning conversations cracking with these clever centerpieces. Fill an egg carton with twelve plastic pull-apart eggs. Inside each egg, put a slip of paper on which you've written a special question such as "What do you hope to accomplish this year?"

or "What special hope has God given you?" If plastic eggs are scarce, use permanent markers to write the questions on hard-boiled eggs.

★ Set party tables with white paper plates. Set yellow cups in the centers of the plates to resemble sunny-side up eggs. Add yellow crepe-paper streamers and balloons around the area. Be sure to have fresh coffee brewing and chilled fruit juices available as families arrive. What a welcoming aroma to all who attend your good-morning gala!

★ Party prizes or festival favors might include boxes of pancake mix, colorful paper plates, or plastic spatulas with family names written on them with paint pens.

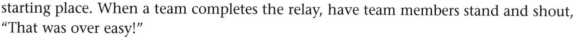

FESTIVAL GAMES

Eggs-Over-Easy Relay

Simple Supplies: You'll need chairs, tape, four pot holders, paper plates, and paper eggs. Make eggs in a sunny-side up design.

Directions: Before the game, tape sunny-side up eggs to both sides of each pot holder. Place chairs in four rows. This relay can be played by up to four families at one time.

Hand each person a paper plate, then form up to four family teams. Have team members sit in the chairs. Hand the first person in each row a pot holder. Explain that players in this rise-and-shine relay will flip the eggs over their heads to the players behind them. Those players must catch the eggs on their plates, then flip them to the people behind them. If an egg is missed, it must be tossed again. Play continues until the eggs have traveled down the line and back to the starting place. When a team completes the relay, have team members stand and shout, "That was over easy!"

When the game is over, point out that it took each family member's help to accomplish the relay. Remind families that God helps us accomplish his will and gives us hope for the future.

Resolution Solution

Simple Supplies: You'll need pencils, paper clips, tape, scissors, and red construction paper. Cut out a large paper heart for each family. Cut each heart into six pieces and paper clip the heart puzzle pieces together.

Directions: Remind families that God is in control of our lives but that he gives us free choice. God wants us to make good choices and to trust in his help to stick with those choices. When we trust God's help, we have hope of changing. Explain that in this activity, everyone will resolve to make one positive change in his life during the new year.

Hand a heart puzzle and several pencils to each family. Invite each person to choose a puzzle piece and on it write a resolution for the coming year. Adults may need to help young children write their resolutions. Resolutions might include spending more time with families, working harder in school, or being more patient with siblings.

When family members finish their resolutions, challenge them to assemble the puzzle pieces into a heart and tape them together. When the heart puzzles are complete, have family members shout, "We hope for God's help in the new year!" Remind everyone that God helps us because he loves us. And with God's help, we can hope to accomplish our resolutions. Encourage families to take their hopeful hearts home and hang them in a place where they'll be seen often.

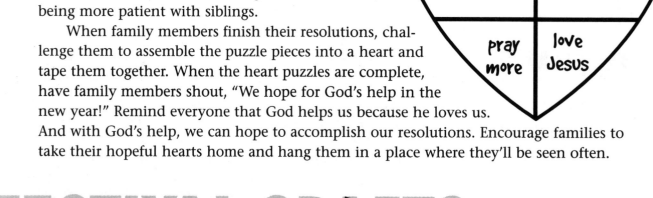

FESTIVAL CRAFTS

Express Yourself Paints

Simple Supplies: You'll need newspapers, cornstarch, clear liquid dishwashing soap, plastic spoons, food coloring, quart-sized resealable plastic freezer bags, and damp washcloths for cleanup.

Directions: Have families briefly discuss ways they experience hope in their lives every day. Some examples might include hoping for sunny days, hoping for good health, or hoping the dentist doesn't call to remind them of a checkup! Point out that everyday hope colors our lives with trust, faith, and love. Then explain that families will be making special paints to express the joy in having everyday hope.

Cover a table with newspapers and set out the food coloring, cornstarch, plastic spoons, and clear dishwashing soap. Hand a resealable plastic bag to each person. Measure 2 spoonfuls each of the cornstarch and dishwashing soap into the plastic bag. Seal the bag and squeeze it gently to combine the ingredients. Then open the bag and add several drops of food coloring. Reseal the bag and gently knead the ingredients together to form opaque paints. Family members may each want to make a different color of paint so they'll have a colorful variety. As families work, encourage them to talk about the hopes they have for each day and for the coming year.

Invite families to take their paints home to decorate joy-filled "stained glass" windows, or designate a window at church for families to cooperatively paint. If there's time, cover a table with newspapers, then let families paint their jars from the Sweet Hope Coffeecake activity, small white ceramic tiles, or pictures on paper. Provide cotton swabs to use as paintbrushes.

Sweet Hope Coffeecake

Simple Supplies: *You'll need unsweetened cocoa, sugar, flour, baking powder, chocolate chips, salt, measuring cups, measuring spoons, chopped walnuts (optional), tape, and a pint jar with lid for each family. You'll also need a photocopy of the recipe card below for each family.*

Directions: Remind families that hope springs from our love of God and that each new day begins with the sweetness of hope and renewal. Explain to families that they'll make edible crafts to bake and share at home to remind them of the sweet hope each day brings.

Hand each family a recipe card and a pint jar with lid. Have families work together to measure the dry ingredients into the jars. As you add the ingredients, gently tap the jar to compact the layers. Replace the lids, then tape the recipe cards to the outsides of the jars. Tell families that the Sweet Hope Coffeecakes are now ready to bake for tomorrow morning's breakfast.

Sweet Hope Coffee Cake

- **At Church:** In a jar, add these ingredients in order: 1 cup sugar, 1/4 cup cocoa, 1 cup flour, 1 teaspoon baking powder, 1/2 teaspoon salt. Sprinkle on 1/4 cup of chocolate chips and, if available, 1/4 cup of walnuts. Place the lid on the jar.

- **At home:** Preheat the oven to 350 degrees. Spray a 9-by-13-inch pan with non-stick coating. Pour the dry ingredients into a large mixing bowl. Add 3 eggs and 3/4 cup cooking oil or applesauce, then stir until well blended. Pour the batter into a prepared pan and bake for 25 minutes or until done. When the cake cools, cut it into 24 pieces.

FESTIVAL FOOD

It's-in-the-Bag Eggs and Toast

Simple Supplies: *You'll need uncooked eggs, heavy-duty quart-sized resealable plastic bags, salt and pepper, napkins, paper plates, permanent markers, a large cooking pot, bread, plastic knives and forks, butter, peanut butter (optional), jelly, a toaster, and access to a stove or hot plate.*

Directions: With a few simple ingredients and some boiling water, your celebration breakfast is "in the bag"!

Fill a large cooking pot half full of water and heat it to a gentle boil. Hand a resealable plastic bag to each person. Invite people to crack one or two eggs into their bags, to seal the bags securely, and to write their initials on the bags with permanent markers. Have participants gently knead or shake their bags to mix the eggs. Place several bags into the boiling water and let them cook about 8 to 10 minutes or until firm. While families wait their turn at boiling the eggs, have them discuss how God helps them find hope and new beginnings in their lives.

While their eggs are cooking, invite families to make toast or peanut butter and jelly sandwiches. When the eggs are done, scrape them onto a paper plate or eat them right from the bag!

FESTIVAL FINALE

Hope for a Change
Simple Supplies: *You'll need Bibles.*

Directions: Invite family groups to sit together. Have families open their Bibles to 2 Thessalonians 2:15-17 and follow along as a volunteer reads the passage aloud. As the passage is being read, encourage family members to pantomime actions for the words of hope in the verses, which include *stand firm, hold, love, hope,* and *encouragement.* Then challenge family groups to discuss one or more of these questions:

★ What hopes does your family have for the new year?
★ How can God's love and help create renewed hope in us?
★ What hopes do you think God has for you this year?

Encourage families to make a list at home of ways they can accomplish changes in their lives this year. Close with a prayer thanking God for his help and for the abundant hope he offers with each new day.

FAMILY FESTIVAL FOLLOW-UP

Heifer Project International

After families have enjoyed their Sweet Hope Coffeecake at home, encourage them to place the empty jars (or even empty egg cartons) on their kitchen tables to encourage them to donate their loose change to a worthwhile project. The Heifer Project gives cows, goats, chickens, pigs, and other animals to poor families in 110 countries around the world. These animals provide eggs, milk, or cheese for many needy families to eat. A gift of about $20 can purchase a whole flock of chickens for a poor third world village, and that's a lot of eggs for breakfast! What a way to instill the hope of food, employment, and pride in poverty-stricken families around the world. For more information, call Heifer Project International at 1-800-422-0474.

SOUPER BOWL PARTY

Celebrate Super Bowl Sunday with an emphasis on compassion for others.

BIBLE BASIS: Luke 10:25-37

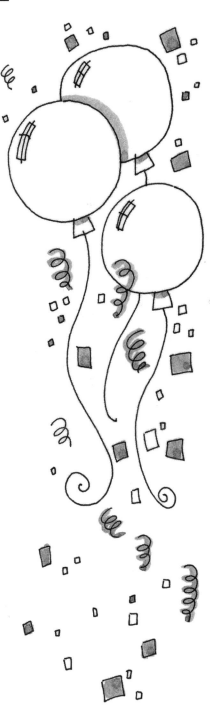

Football is not a sport usually associated with warmth and compassion. Rather, it's a sport filled with crippling competition. To top it off, many teams receive salaries that could feed some third world countries. It's important to keep priorities in balance during this season of rough-and-tumble teams and Super Bowl mania. This year, plan your own church Souper Bowl Party to commemorate compassion and to encourage families to reach out to others in their neighborhood and community who may be hungry, hurt, or homeless.

GETTING READY

Each activity in this family festival contains its own list of simple supplies. Simply choose and use the activities that fit your needs and time requirements, then gather the appropriate supplies. Use one or more of these decorating and invitation suggestions to enliven your special event:

★ Tie photocopied invitations to the handles of plastic soup spoons with curling ribbon.

★ Hang colorful plastic soup spoons and bowls around the room and from the ceiling as unique decorations.

★ Advertise your Souper Bowl Party with a canned food drive prior to the event. Use a clean trash barrel decorated like a soup can to create an eye-catching display. Provide party information and who will benefit from the donations on the label.

★ Simple party prizes and favors might include cans of soup, bags of oyster crackers, or personalized plastic soup bowls.

Feed the Hungry

Simple Supplies: You'll need plastic soup spoons, water, disposable soup bowls, and chairs.

Directions: Remind families that one way we can show compassion to others in need is by sharing our food. Explain that this fun relay will remind us to share food with others.

Direct family teams to stand in lines at one end of the room. Hand each team a soup bowl half full of water, an empty soup bowl, and a plastic soup spoon. Place the bowls containing water on the floor in front of each family line. Have families choose one member to be the receiver and hold the empty bowl. Instruct the receivers to sit in chairs about 10 feet from their family lines.

Festival Finesse

Use packing peanuts if water might cause hard floors to become slippery.

At a starting signal, have the first person from each team dip a spoonful of pretend soup from her bowl and gently carry it to the receiver. Players must empty the soup into the receivers' bowls, then hurry back to their lines, where the next team members repeat the process. Play continues for 3 minutes or until one team fills its receiver's bowl.

When the relay is finished, the team with the most soup in its receiver's bowl wins. Award the winning team (or everyone!) a compassionate pat on the back as a prize.

Helping Hands

Simple Supplies: No supplies required.

Directions: Point out that everyone needs a helping hand once in a while. Ask families to briefly recount the parable of the Good Samaritan, then explain that families will get the chance in this activity to help each other in unusual ways.

Have each person find a partner, then have pairs stand facing each other. Have the festival leader be the Good Samaritan for the first round. The Good Samaritan is to stand in the middle of playing area, clap his hands, and begin chanting, "Hand to hand, hand to hand, we can offer helping hands." As the Good Samaritan chants, partners clap hand to hand. But when the Good Samaritan changes the chant, partners must change their actions. For example, the Good Samaritan might say, "elbow to elbow," "toes to toes," "shoulder to knee," or any other combination. When the Good Samaritan shouts, "Helping Hands," each person, including the Good Samaritan, must find a new partner. The person left without a partner becomes the new Good Samaritan. Play until there have been several changes of partners. End the game by inviting participants to sit in a circle and tell about times someone gave them a helping hand.

The Cracker Bowl

Simple Supplies: You'll need flour, newspapers, salt, powdered alum (available in the spice section of the grocery store), water, large bowls, measuring cups, measuring spoons, and markers.

Directions: These decorated crafts are "souper" cracker bowls—and families will delight in making them!

Cover the work area with newspapers and set out the craft materials. Have each family measure 1 cup of flour, 1 cup of salt, and 1 teaspoon of powdered alum into a large bowl.

Slowly add 1/2 to 2/3 cup of water, kneading and mixing the ingredients until they're a clay-like consistency. Take turns kneading the dough until it's smooth. Divide the clay and let each family member make a small bowl, or design one family-sized bowl to hold lots of oyster crackers, popcorn, or fresh fruit.

Set the bowls on newspapers labeled with each family's name. At the end of the festival, remind families to take their bowls home to air dry. This takes about 24 hours, depending on the size and thickness of the bowls. When dry, the bowls can be painted and sprayed with clear shellac, then used to hold crispy soup crackers.

Festival Finesse

Provide pencils, toothpicks, combs, or other items that will give interesting textures to the clay.

Soup Stones

Simple Supplies: You'll need newspapers, plain-colored 4-inch ceramic tiles, permanent markers or paint pens, and self-adhesive felt dots (available in hardware departments). Get free ceramic tiles from builders with extras, or try contacting a home decorating store for tile samples or leftovers.

Directions: Explain to families that trivets hold hot bowls of soup and other foods to protect the tables they sit on. Point out that protection is one way God shows his compassion for us. Explain that families will be making Soup Stone trivets to remind everyone that compassion is an expression of love and caring.

Cover the work area with newspapers. Hand each family member a ceramic tile. Challenge families to draw pictures or write words that illustrate compassion or caring deeds. Suggest that they draw scenes from the parable of the Good Samaritan or of times Jesus helped others. (You may wish to provide young artists with old shirts to protect their clothing.) As families work, encourage them to tell ways we can show compassion and love to others.

When the Soup Stones are decorated, glue four felt dots to the bottom of each trivet so it won't scratch wooden surfaces.

FESTIVAL FOOD

Compassion Soup

Simple Supplies: You'll need very hot water, instant rice, chicken bouillon, dehydrated minced chives or dried parsley, napkins, plastic spoons, crackers, and large Styrofoam cups.

Directions: Have each family member measure and pour into her cup 2 spoonfuls of instant rice, 1 spoonful of chicken bouillon, and 1 spoonful of dehydrated minced chives or dried parsley flakes. Designate an adult or teen volunteer to carefully fill each cup half full of very hot water. Gently stir the soup, then let it stand for 5 minutes or until the rice is soft. Serve the cup of soup you've made to another member in your family, then sit and sip together as you share ways of showing compassion to others who may be hungry or needy. Serve crispy soup crackers with your treat.

FESTIVAL FINALE

Compassion for Others

Simple Supplies: You'll need a Bible, scrap paper, shiny pennies, and an empty soup-can bank for each family.

Directions: Invite family groups to form small circles. Hand each family member two pennies. Tell families that they'll help retell the parable of the Good Samaritan to end the festival. Explain that this was a story Jesus told to explain how God wants us to show compassion to people who are in need. Read the following aloud as you lead families in the accompanying actions.

A man was walking from Jerusalem to Jericho (walk in place) **when he fell into the hands of robbers. The robbers stole the man's money, then left him hurt on the side of the road. Mean, nasty robbers!** (Shake your finger.) **The poor man groaned and moaned.** (Make moaning noises.) **Who would help him?**

A priest came walking down the road (walk in place)**, but when he saw the man, the priest passed by on the other side. He didn't stop. Oh dear** (sadly shake your head)**, would anyone help the hurt man? Then a Levite came walking along** (walk in place)**, but the Levite passed by too. Oh dear** (sadly shake your head)**, would anyone help the hurt man? Then a man from Samaria came riding a donkey.** (Trot and make clip-clop noises with your tongue.) **Would he stop? He did! This good Samaritan bandaged the man's wounds, offered him water, and took him to town on his donkey.** (Trot and make clip-clop noises with your tongue.) **The good Samaritan even paid for the man to be cared for!** (Place your pennies in the center of each family circle.)

When Jesus was done with his story, he asked, "Which of these three do you think was a neighbor to the man who fell into the hands of robbers: the priest, the Levite, or the Samaritan?"

Ask families to answer Jesus' question and to point out ways the Samaritan showed compassion to the injured man. Encourage families to read Luke 10:36-37 together at home. Then close with a prayer asking God to give each person a spirit of compassion and a willingness to share with others who are in need. Distribute the empty soup-can banks so each family can place their pennies inside. Challenge families to collect coins until their banks are full, then donate the money to a local service organization.

FAMILY FESTIVAL FOLLOW-UP

Lend a Helping Hand

Show compassion for others by donating the canned food from your church's canned-food drive to a local soup kitchen or food pantry. You may wish to include decorated plastic soup bowls on which you've written "Love your neighbor as yourself" (Matthew 19:19). Contact the soup kitchen or food pantry prior to your delivery and ask if they could use a few extra helping hands to make, serve, or clean up meals. Most soup kitchens or food pantries are always looking for compassionate workers to pitch in!

Family Faith Builder:

Friendship

FRIENDS FESTIVAL

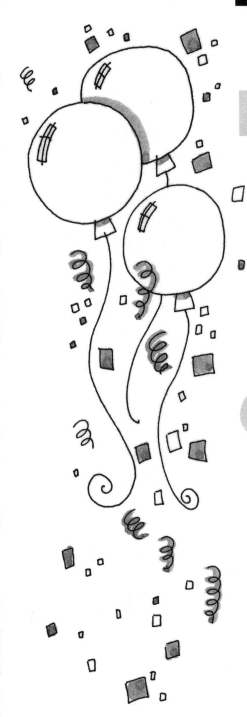

Learn qualities that make friendships fantastic!

BIBLE BASIS: 1 Samuel 18:1-4; 19:1-7

Friendship is common to life and essential to happiness the world over. By developing friendships with others around the world, we gain an appreciation for different cultures and traditions. We also gain an understanding of our relationship with God and how we can share his special friendship with others. Families will make unique memories sharing this festival of friends from around the world—and may even develop a lasting friendship with one of God's children in another country through the Family Festival Follow-Up activity.

GETTING READY

Each activity in this family festival contains its own list of simple supplies. Simply choose and use the activities that fit your needs and time requirements, then gather the appropriate supplies. Use one or more of these decorating and invitation suggestions to enliven your special event:

★ Arrange a Heritage Potluck to announce your special event. Invite families to supply portions of the meal from their own family cookbooks and cultural traditions. A big bowl of spaghetti tastes extra yummy when served with taco salad!

★ Cut out multicolored gingerbread-shaped people to use as invitations to the Friends Festival. If your group of families is small, consider attaching colorful invitation notes to edible gingerbread men.

★ Visit your local library and check out music from different countries. Play the festive melodies while families are arriving or during the entire Friends Festival.

18

★ Decorate your celebration space in an eclectic fashion. Ask families to bring ethnic decorations, such as large sombreros, Chinese chopsticks, Swedish clogs, or colorful piñatas.

★ Party favors might include world maps, tiny compasses, friendship rings, or bracelets.

FESTIVAL GAMES

Escargot Hopscotch (France)

Simple Supplies: You'll need masking tape or chalk and game markers such as stones, pennies, or beanbags. This game requires a large play area.

Directions: Before the festival, use masking tape to create the large snail-shaped game outline with numbers. Add a masking-tape tossing line 2 feet from the first square. If you are playing outside, use chalk to draw the game outline and tossing line on a sidewalk.

Tell families that escargot (es car GO), or snail, is a food that friends in France often share. Explain that children in France even play a game on a snail-shaped pattern with their friends as they learn how to cooperate with each other.

Festival Finesse

If your group is very large, form teams of no more than twelve people or less. You may want to have one or two groups play Escargot Hopscotch while the remaining groups play another game or make a festival craft. Then have the groups rotate to the remaining activities.

Have players find partners and hand each pair a game marker. Invite the first pair to stand behind the tossing line. Explain that the game is played much like hopscotch, but in this game partners must help each other hop on one foot with elbows linked or arms around each other's waists. Partners will toss their marker onto the snail board, then hop around the snail and back without touching any lines or hopping onto a square with a game marker on it. Direct partners to leave their marker in place as the next pair tosses its game marker on the board.

By the end of the game, the snail will have lots of markers on it, so partners will need to brainstorm and plan their strategy for tossing and hopping. The last pair to hop around without landing on a line or a square with a marker on it wins the game.

When the game is finished, gather players in a line and have them give the people next to them a friendly handshake. Continue holding hands as you wind the line into a snail pattern. Then have players pray for children in France, especially those who may not know God as their friend.

Pin (Guatemala)

Simple Supplies: You'll need masking tape, several empty milk jugs, and the sack balls made in the festival crafts. You'll need a large playing area for this game.

Directions: Make two masking-tape lines on the floor about 20 feet apart. Place milk jug "pins" between the two lines and about 5 feet apart.

Explain that friends in Guatemala play this game for fun and to learn cooperation. Play Pin to remind families that friends cooperate and communicate.

Form family teams and have them stand in lines behind the tape boundaries. Each member should have a sack ball. The first player in each line rolls her ball toward one of the pins, trying to get the ball close to the pin without knocking it over. The rest of the family members on the team take turns rolling their sack balls at the first ball. The object is to hit the first ball closer and closer to the pin until it's touching the pin. If the first ball rolled is not touching the pin when everyone has rolled their sack balls, players can roll their balls again.

When the first ball is finally touching the pin, the game is over and all family members are winners. If the pin is knocked over, the player who knocked it over stands the pin up, rolls a ball, and the game begins again.

When game time is over, have each group of players form a circle and give friendly pats on the backs to the team members next to them. Encourage people to pray for the people of Guatemala who must live in a war-torn country.

X	X	X	X
X	X	X	X
X	X	X	X

family rolling line

O   O   O   O   O

X	X	X	X
X	X	X	X
X	X	X	X

FESTIVAL CRAFTS

Sack Balls (Zimbabwe)

Simple Supplies: You'll need six plastic grocery bags and one rubber band for each ball. You'll also need permanent markers and scissors.

Directions: Point out to families that toys are so expensive in Zimbabwe that children and their friends use discarded grocery bags to make their own toys.

Hand each family member six plastic bags and a rubber band. Instruct everyone to open one grocery bag, then crumple and push the remaining five bags inside. Remove excess air by running your hand down the bag and compacting the bags inside to create a round ball. Wrap a rubber band tightly around the outer bag, just above the ball. Cut off the extra plastic 1 inch above the rubber band. Invite family members to decorate the outsides of the sack balls with permanent markers. As families work, discuss qualities of friendship, such as honesty, loyalty, caring, and helpfulness. Point out that God gives us good friends and wants us to treat them as special gifts.

When the sack balls are complete, invite people to stand in a circle and toss the balls to each other as they name things friends can share, such as fun, help, dreams, troubles, and especially God. End the craft activity by praying for the children of Zimbabwe who may not have much time to play because they must work to support their families.

Friendship Pins (America)

Simple Supplies: You'll need large safety pins, needle-nose pliers, and colorful seed beads (available at craft stores).

Directions: Explain that families may come in all shapes and sizes but that happy families all have one thing in common—they're friends! Tell participants they'll be making friendship pins to exchange with members of their own family and other families as well.

Have each family gather in a small circle on the floor. In the middle of each family circle, place a small container of seed beads and ten to fifteen safety pins. If possible, have a pair of needle-nose pliers available for each family. Designate one family member to use the pliers to slightly spread the small circle at the bottom of each safety pin so the beads will slide on easily. Have family members decide on a distinctive pattern of five to six beads. Slide the beads down and around the small circle so they remain on the long sides of the pins. Encourage families to assign a quality of friendship to each color. For example, red might signify love, while blue might stand for compassion. Have each person make at least two friendship pins.

When the pins are finished, use the pliers to squeeze the small circles closed. Exchange one set of friendship pins within your own family and the second set of pins with another family. Fasten your colorful pins to tennis shoes, shoelaces, shirts, backpacks, or even key chains. Try connecting several pins together to create a unique fashion statement!

FESTIVAL FOOD

Friends Pizza (Italy)

Simple Supplies: You'll need flour tortillas, canned pizza sauce, shredded mozzarella cheese, napkins, paper plates, and plastic spoons.

Directions: Remind families that pizza, a classic Italian food, can be made in a jiffy to leave plenty of time to enjoy eating it with family and friends!

Have participants wash their hands. Then give each person one flour tortilla, explaining that the round tortilla can symbolize a friend's love, which goes round and round in an unending circle. Using the spoons, spread a small amount of room temperature pizza sauce on top of each tortilla. Point out that spreading the sauce reminds us how friends can spread their love and God's love to others. Sprinkle the mozzarella cheese over the top as you tell everyone that friends generously sprinkle their friendships with help, understanding, and encouragement. Gently roll up the tortillas, jellyroll style, and eat them while discussing what qualities each person likes in a friend.

FESTIVAL FINALE

Friends Forever!

Simple Supplies: You'll need Bibles.

Invite family groups to each find a quiet place to sit together. Remind families that the Bible has wonderful examples of God-centered friendships such as Ruth and Naomi and Paul and Timothy. Explain that you'll end your friendship festival by learning more about another God-centered friendship between David and Jonathan. Have families open their Bibles to 1 Samuel 18:1-4; 19:1-7 and read along as a volunteer reads the passage aloud. Then ask everyone to point out ways in which David and Jonathan exemplified friendship. Finally, challenge family groups to think about and discuss one or more of these questions:

★ How is friendship shown within your family? to others?

★ Think about your own friendships. Which friends have led you closer to God? How?

★ How can being a friend improve our relationships with others? with God?

Close with a prayer thanking God for friendships in our families, with other families, and with others around the world. Be sure to thank God for his perfect friendship and love!

FAMILY FESTIVAL FOLLOW-UP

Compassion International

What better way for your family to develop friendships with children around the world than to sponsor a child in another country through Compassion International? Your friendship and gift of money helps provide children in other countries with improved education, better health, personal encouragement, and positive interaction with Christian adults. For more information, call 1-800-336-7676 or write to:

Compassion International
Colorado Springs, CO 80997

JUBILEE OF LOVE

Family Faith Builder:

Christian love

Celebrate Valentine's Day with an emphasis on Christian love.

BIBLE BASIS: 1 Corinthians 13:4-8

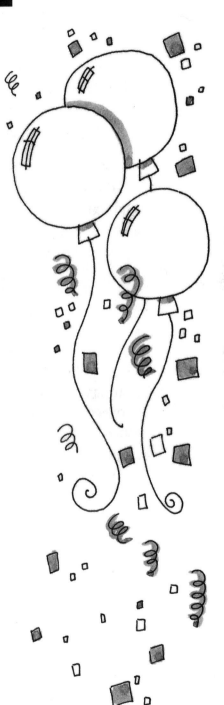

What does Christian love mean? It's not the same as loving chocolate, loving to sleep late, or even loving Valentine's Day. Christian love is love in action! It's more than just a warm feeling inside. It's putting that feeling to work to show kindness, patience, humility, and perseverance. This year, celebrate Valentine's Day by putting love into action using the perfect model of Christian love from 1 Corinthians 13.

GETTING READY

Each activity in this family festival contains its own list of simple supplies. Simply choose and use the activities that fit your needs and time requirements, then gather the appropriate supplies. Use one or more of these decorating and invitation suggestions to enliven your special event:

★ Have you ever wondered what to do with all of those sugary candy conversation hearts? Put 'em to use on clever invitations! Glue several candy hearts to a large construction paper heart. On the back of the heart, put the date and time of your festival and instructions to create a family "love poem," using the words on the candy hearts somewhere in the text. Invite people to bring the poems for display at the festival.

★ As people arrive for the festival, have supplies available for each person to create a unique Valentine's card. Don't forget to have artists sign their names on the backs of the cards! Have each person write her name on a small slip of paper and place the paper in a decorated container such as a frilly candy box. At the end of the festival, each person can draw a name and present her card to that person.

★ Suspend a variety of paper hearts and streamers around the festival area. Go colorfully beyond traditional Valentine colors and use whimsical blue, purple, and orange hearts! You may also want to write one of the qualities mentioned in 1 Corinthians 13:4-8 on each of the hearts. Use words such as patience and kindness.

★ Party favors and prizes might include small boxes of candy hearts, a box of Valentine cards, or chocolate candy kisses.

FESTIVAL GAMES

Love Action Addition
Simple Supplies: *No supplies required.*

Directions: Remind families that there are many ways to express affection and love to each other. In this expressive game, families will discover that it's fun to put affection—and warm hugs—into action!

Form family circles. If a family has only a few members, invite them to join another family to create a larger circle. Have one person in each group begin with an action that shows affection and love to the person next to him. This could be a hug, a squeeze of the hand, a pat on the shoulder, or even blowing a kiss. The next player repeats the action and adds one of her own. Continue repeating and adding actions around the circle. When the sequence of actions becomes too long to remember, end with a family hug.

For a lively challenge, have group members affirm each other with loving expressions as they add new actions. For example, you might give a squeeze of the hand and say, "You're so kind to others," or "You're a great mom!" Remember to repeat both actions and words every time a player adds new ones. This version of the game will get players giggling as they affirm others with expressions meant for someone else!

Pass the Love, Please
Simple Supplies: *You'll need two sandwich bags filled with twenty-four candy hearts for every two or three families. You'll also need to provide lively music.*

Directions: Young family members will especially love this simple game, and everyone will learn that telling others about God's love is a way to show we care!

Invite two or three families to join and form a sitting circle. Hand each group two sandwich bags containing candy hearts. Explain that this game is played a bit like musical chairs. When the music begins, players are to pass the bags of hearts around the circle as quickly as possible. When the music stops, each player holding a bag removes a candy, presents it to someone in the circle, and says, "God loves you." Then close the bags and begin the music again. Play until each person has at least one candy heart and has given away a heart.

After the game, talk about the value of telling others about God's love. Point out that when we share God's love with others, we show how much we care for them. Encourage family members to tell someone at the festival that God loves them.

FESTIVAL CRAFTS

Perpetual Valentines

Simple Supplies: *You'll need newspapers, markers, crayons, stickers, glitter glue, old Valentine cards, clear Con-Tact paper, lace doilies, several shades of lipstick, Tacky craft glue, scissors, and a 4-inch poster-board heart for each person.*

Directions: Cover a table with newspaper and set out the craft supplies. Tell families that Christian love means showing our love all year round, not just during special holidays such as Valentine's Day. Explain that families will be making beautiful Valentine cards to hide and then discover at home all through the year as a constant reminder of family love.

Hand each person a paper heart and invite everyone to use the craft supplies to create a beautiful card. For a whimsical touch, let participants use their fingers to rub a bit of lipstick on their lips and then "kiss" their Valentines. Be sure to have people write their names on the backs of the cards. When the Valentine hearts are finished, cover them in clear Con-Tact paper.

Encourage family members to take their Valentines home and hide them throughout the house. When someone discovers a card in its hiding spot, she is to give the Valentine's creator a hug, then hide the Valentine again. You'll keep sharing your love all year with this fun game of Valentine hide-and-seek!

Lil' Bit of Love Coupons

Simple Supplies: *You'll need candy conversation hearts, old Valentine cards or wrapping paper, construction paper, markers, Tacky craft glue, scissors, and newspapers. You'll also need ten 1-by-3-inch slips of paper and a clean empty soup can without the label for each family. Be sure to smooth any rough edges on the can.*

Directions: Cover a table with newspapers and set out the craft materials. Explain that families will be making fun family coupon holders to help them put their love into action.

Hand each family group an empty soup can. Invite families to decorate their soup cans with wrapping paper, old Valentine cards, markers, and construction paper. They may also wish to glue candy conversation hearts to the outsides of the cans. Then have each family make ten coupons on the slips of paper. These coupons should promise loving gestures such as, "I'll read the family a story," "I'll clear the table," "Good for one family hug," or "I'll say something kind to my family today."

Place the coupons in the cans and encourage family members to take turns drawing coupons out of the can at breakfast. At dinner, family members can tell how they fulfilled the coupons during the day. Place the coupons back in the can to be drawn again.

FESTIVAL FOOD

Sweetheart Fondue

Simple Supplies: You'll need chocolate syrup or fudge topping, three-ringed pretzels, cake decorating sprinkles, napkins, and two small disposable bowls for each family. You may also want damp paper towels for cleaning up any sticky fingers or tables!

Directions: Gather families around their own "fondue pots" to share dipped pretzels and loving conversation.

Have each family pour about a quarter cup of chocolate sauce or fudge topping in one of their bowls and several tablespoons of decorating sprinkles in the other bowl. Let family members take turns quickly dipping their pretzels in the chocolate or fudge sauce, then dipping them in the colorful sprinkles. As the special treats are nibbled, point out how the pretzels look a bit like hearts. Encourage people to talk about why they think the heart is used as a symbol of love and how they show love to each other and to others.

FESTIVAL FINALE

Love Is. . .

Simple Supplies: You'll need Bibles.

Directions: Invite family groups to find quiet places to sit. Have family members open their Bibles to 1 Corinthians 13:4-8 and follow along as a volunteer reads the passage aloud. Have each family join with another family to discuss the following questions:

★ Which qualities of Christian love described in 1 Corinthians 13 do you find the easiest to show to others? Explain.

★ How does showing others our love demonstrate our love for the Lord?

★ What can we as a family do this week to show someone our love?

Close the festival by prayerfully singing this song to the tune of "Jesus Loves Me."

Jesus loves us, this we know,

For the Bible tells us so.

We can show his love to all—

Love to others, big and small.

Yes, Jesus loves us.

Yes, Jesus loves us.

Yes, Jesus loves us.

The Bible tells us so.

Love Letters

Challenge families to make and send cards or letters to sick children around the United States. Focus the letters and cards on a general theme of happiness and love instead of get well wishes (since some children may be terminally ill). Place your love notes in stamped envelopes that are open and not addressed. Then place those envelopes inside a large stamped envelope and mail it to:

Love Letters
436A Eisenhower Lane
Lombard, IL 60148

Family Faith Builder:

Spreading God's Word

SAINT PAT'S PARTY

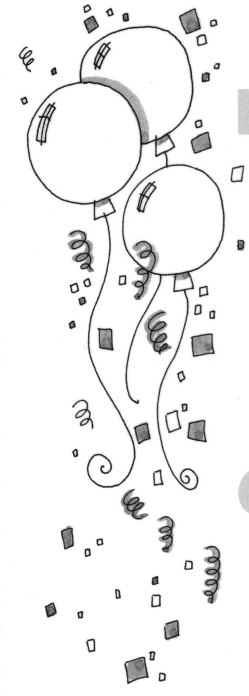

Triumph in the lives of St. Patrick and St. Stephen in this not-so-traditional festival.

BIBLE BASIS: Acts 7:54-60

Saint Patrick's Day is a day filled with green shamrocks, blarney stones, and leprechauns. But who was St. Patrick, and why do we have a holiday to celebrate his life? St. Patrick introduced Christianity into Ireland during the fifth century and used the shamrock to teach new believers about the Trinity. For Christians in Ireland, Saint Patrick's Day isn't a day to talk about good luck and leprechauns, but one filled with religious festivities and the Lord.

This special St. Pat's Party also centers around the life of another loyal servant of God, Stephen. Stephen's life could have been an example for St. Patrick, for Stephen was an early Christian leader who taught people about Jesus' life, death, and resurrection. Celebrate the "wearing of the green" this year with a tribute to two loyal saints of God who spread the good news to others.

GETTING READY

Each activity in this family festival contains its own list of simple supplies. Simply choose and use the activities that fit your needs and time requirements, then gather the appropriate supplies. Use one or more of these decorating and invitation suggestions to enliven your special event:

★ Staple three small green paper plates together to form shamrocks. Write "You're Invited!" on one of the leaves. Then photocopy your party information on green paper and glue the invitation to another leaf. Finally, write "Bring another family!" on the third leaf.

★ If families are able, have each bring a bag of small green lollipops. If they're not able to find bags with only green lollipops, other colors will work. (This information could be written on the festival invitations.)

★ Make your room gleam with green, the traditional color of Saint Patrick's Day. Place greenery on tables to symbolize eternal life and the coming of spring. Encourage families to come to the festival "wearin' the green." Cut out bushels of green three-leaf shamrocks and scatter them on tables and floors. These shamrocks can be used by party participants in the Festival Finale.

★ Tie green balloons in groups of three to symbolize the shamrock and its representation of the Trinity. Hang these airy "shamrocks" around the party room.

★ Party prizes and favors could include green items such as combs, erasers, sour-apple candies, small notepads, and pencils.

FESTIVAL GAMES

Praise Phrase

Simple Supplies: You'll need newspapers, clear packing tape, markers, the Good News Trail Mix bags from the Festival Food activity, and one large brown paper bag for each family.

Directions: Gather families and briefly explain that Stephen was an early Christian who loved Jesus very much and wanted others to know, love, and follow him too. Stephen spent his life telling others the good news about Jesus. Explain that in this game, family members will get a chance to tell good news about Jesus too.

Have each family place its bags of Good News Trail Mix in the bottom of a paper bag, stuff several crumpled newspapers around the snacks, and tape the bag shut. Suggest that each family write their last name on the bag. Instruct family members to stand in a circle. Explain that this game is played like volleyball, except each time the bag is volleyed to another family member, that person must say the name of a person he or she could tell about Jesus or call out a praise phrase about Jesus, such as "Jesus is Lord" or "Jesus can save us."

As the bags begin to deteriorate, have families tear them open piñata-style and munch the goodies inside. You may wish to provide chilled fruit juice or lemonade with the treats. Encourage families to discuss why it's important to tell others about Jesus as Stephen did. Then have families clean up the area before moving to the next activity.

> **Festival Finesse**
> You may wish to begin your event by making the Good News Trail Mix in the Festival Food section. You'll need this snack for the first festival game.

St. Patrick Says

Simple Supplies: No supplies required.

Directions: Explain to families that St. Patrick first introduced Christianity to the people of Ireland during the fifth century. He told people about Jesus and how to follow him.

Explain to players that this is a "following" game played much like Simon Says. Choose someone to lead the game as St. Patrick. The leader should be able to give directions quickly to make the game lively and to keep everyone on her toes! The rest of the players will be followers.

Have St. Patrick stand facing the followers. As in Simon Says, everyone follows the directions and actions of the leader, but only when the leader says, "St. Patrick says..." In this game, however, players who are eliminated are to hold the hand of a family member or friend and continue in the game. The game ends when everyone is joined together. End with high fives, then say a prayer asking Jesus for help in joining others to him.

FESTIVAL CRAFTS

Trinity Shamrock Pop-Pins

Simple Supplies: *You'll need green and white curling ribbon, scissors, clear packing tape, large safety pins, and three green (or assorted colors of) lollipops for each person.*

Directions: Tell families that St. Patrick is not mentioned in the Bible but that he loved and followed God and told others about God, Jesus, and the Holy Spirit. St. Patrick also used the three-leafed shamrock to teach new believers about the Trinity. Briefly explain how your church views the union of the Father, Son, and Holy Spirit. Then tell families they'll be making tasty shamrock pins to remind them of how St. Patrick told others about God, Jesus, and the Holy Spirit.

Have each person arrange three lollipops to form a shamrock. Use clear packing tape to fasten the lollipops together across the cellophane wrappers on one side of each shamrock. Tape a large safety pin in the center of the packing tape. Finally, tie green and white ribbon bows around the sticks. Pin the Trinity Shamrock Pop-Pins to shirts, shoes, or jackets.

As families work, point out how the shamrock has three leaves joined in one clover. This reminds us of how the Father, Son, and Holy Spirit are joined in one power. Encourage families to make two extra shamrock pins to be donated to residents at a care center or a kids' hospital on Saint Patrick's Day.

Trinity Bookmarks

Simple Supplies: *You'll need clear Con-Tact paper, paper punches, markers, scissors, green silk cord or ribbon, and green construction paper.*

Directions: Before the festival, cut a 6-inch square of Con-Tact paper for each person. Leave the paper backing in place. You may wish to cut shamrock shapes out of the construction paper ahead of time or leave this for parents and older children to do for themselves and the younger children. You can make great patterns by tracing around a small shamrock-shaped cookie cutter on lightweight cardboard.

Explain to families that both St. Patrick and Stephen served God by bringing his Word to others and by telling others about Jesus. Remind everyone that God's Word is the Bible. Then tell families that they'll make special bookmarks to remind them that they can bring God's Word to others too.

Hand each person a shamrock or have them use a pattern to cut one out of construction paper. Then have family members write one word that describes St. Patrick or St. Stephen on each shamrock. Words might include *loyal, serving, faithful,* and *courageous.*

Next, peel the paper backing off the Con-Tact paper. Arrange a shamrock-shaped cutout on one half of the sticky side of the Con-Tact paper. Carefully fold the Con-Tact paper in half, sticky sides together, to create a Trinity Bookmark. Trim any excess Con-Tact paper from the shamrock, then punch a hold about 1 inch from the top of each shamrock. Thread a 10-inch length of green cord or ribbon through the hole, then knot the ends. Encourage families to use their Trinity Bookmarks in their Bibles.

FESTIVAL FOOD

Good News Trail Mix

Simple Supplies: You'll need resealable plastic sandwich bags, bathroom-sized paper cups, large bowls or paper grocery sacks, and each of the following food items: Lucky Charms cereal, pretzel sticks, chocolate chips, dry roasted peanuts, and small cheese-flavored crackers. You'll also want chilled fruit juice or lemonade.

Directions: Remind families how St. Patrick and Stephen spread the good news about Jesus. As they walked many miles to tell others the good news, they may have munched berries, nuts, and other small foods along the way.

Pour each of the ingredients into a separate bowl or paper sack, then hand each person a resealable plastic sandwich bag and a cup. Invite participants to go down the assembly line and put one cup of each ingredient into their plastic bags. Seal the plastic bags and gently shake them. Munch the trail mix now or save it to use during the Praise Phrase game in the Festival Games section. Use the paper cups for chilled fruit juice or lemonade.

FESTIVAL FINALE

Tell the News!

Simple Supplies: You'll need Bibles, markers, and the green construction-paper shamrock cutouts used as decorations. Be sure there's a shamrock for each person.

Invite family groups to find quiet places to sit together. Have families open their Bibles to Matthew 28:18-20 and follow along as a volunteer reads the passage aloud. Then invite groups to discuss each of these questions:

★ Why is it important to tell others about Jesus?

★ What things might you tell someone about Jesus?

★ Who is one person you could tell about Jesus this week?

Hand each person a shamrock and a marker. Have people write the following on the leaves: "Therefore go and make disciples of all nations" (Matthew 28:19). Challenge participants to tell someone about Jesus this week and then hand that person the shamrock to pass on to someone else along with the good news about Jesus. Close with a prayer asking God to help families serve him by telling others about Jesus' love and forgiveness, just as St. Patrick and Stephen did.

FAMILY FESTIVAL FOLLOW-UP

The Gideons International

Just as St. Patrick and Stephen spread God's Word through their ministries, The Gideons International has served God by placing Bibles in 172 countries around the world for nearly 100 years. If you'd like more information about the Gideons or about how your family can become involved in placing Bibles, write to:

The Gideons International
2900 Lebanon Road
Nashville, Tennessee 37214

COLORS OF SPRING FLING

Family Faith Builder:

Trust

Shower your guests with activities based on the story of Noah and his trust in God.

BIBLE BASIS: Genesis 9:7-17

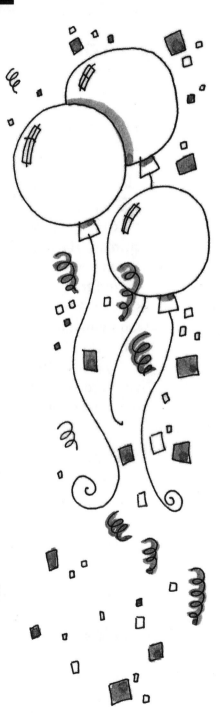

Spring has arrived! And since it is one of God's seasons, we trust that spring and its glorious beauty will arrive each year. We trust that trees and plants will sprout and flowers will bloom. Noah was a man of trust too. Noah trusted God when he built the ark. He trusted God to keep everyone on the ark safe. And just like Noah, families can learn to trust God's loving care and promises. Put your trust in God and celebrate the season with this sunny spring fling.

GETTING READY

Each activity in this family festival contains its own list of simple supplies. Simply choose and use the activities that fit your needs and time requirements, then gather the appropriate supplies. Use one or more of these decorating and invitation suggestions to enliven your special event:

★ To inform families of your event, attach photocopied invitations to flower seed packets.

★ If the budget allows, purchase several containers of flowering bedding plants. Slide the plastic flower containers into festive paper cups and place them around the room and as table centerpieces. When your festival is over, plant the flowers around the church or give them away as door prizes.

★ Create a balloon rainbow over the entrance to your festival. Attach rows of colored balloons to an arch made of sturdy gauge wire and anchored to the door frame with duct tape.

★ Skittles, rainbow-colored candies, can be sprinkled on party tables for a colorful touch and a tasty treat!

★ Festival favors and prizes might include silk flowers, small potted plants, flower seeds, or plastic shovels and watering cans.

FESTIVAL GAMES

Ark Animals

Simple Supplies: No supplies required.

Directions: Remind families of the trust Noah had when he rode on the crowded ark! Then explain that they'll play a fun version of hide-and-seek to remind them of life aboard the ark. Play this game inside or outside on a sunny day.

Designate the boundaries of this game. If you're playing inside a building, designate several rooms as acceptable places to hide. If you're playing outside, set definite out-of-bounds areas. You may wish to pair young children with adults to play this fun game.

Choose one family member to be Noah. The other members of each family will be ark animals. Have each Noah find a place to hide while everyone else closes his eyes and slowly repeats the alphabet. When the alphabet has been said, the family ark animals try to find their Noah. When Noah is found by one of the ark animals, that person must squeeze into the same hiding space with Noah and remain hidden as both wait for other family members to discover them. If another family's Noah is found, keep searching without a word!

When all the members of a family are squeezed on the "ark," shout: "We're all here, and God is near!" While families are huddled together, encourage them to pray and thank God for his loving care.

Trusty Rainbow Golf

Simple Supplies: You'll need markers, masking tape, paper, and the Trusty Rainbows from the craft activity. If you choose not to make the craft, provide a colored plastic lid for each person.

Directions: Before the game, write the numbers 1 to 9 on eighteen sheets of paper, one number per sheet. Then write the names of animals on one set of numbered papers, one animal per sheet. Papers with numbers on them will be the golf tees, while the others will be the golf cups. If your group is very large, make several sets of papers and set up two or three golf courses in different areas. Fasten the papers throughout the playing area, leaving at least 6 feet between tees and cups and trying not to place sequential numbers next to each other.

Have families choose a tee to begin at. Explain that the object of the game is to toss the Trusty Rainbows at the golf cups and count the number of family tosses until one rainbow lands touching the paper. Then all the family members must make the noise of the animal named on the paper. Continue traveling around the course and tossing the rainbows. Keep track of how many tosses are needed on each hole. When every family has completed the course, compare scores and sound effects just for fun. You may want to award all the players with boxes of animals crackers as prizes.

FESTIVAL CRAFTS

Trusty Rainbows

Simple Supplies: For each Trusty Rainbow, you'll need tape and eight 3-inch squares of bright neon card stock.

Directions: Remind families that God put a rainbow in the sky as his promise never to flood the whole world again. Point out that we can always trust God's promises. Then explain that families will be making their own rainbows as colorful reminders of God's trustworthy promises.

To make each Trusty Rainbow, fold one square of colored paper in half so the crease is at the top. Then fold down the upper left corner to the bottom center of the rectangle to form a triangle-shaped pocket. Fold up the lower right corner to the top center to form an open triangle. The paper should now be in the shape of a parallelogram. Repeat the process with the other seven squares.

To assemble each Trusty Rainbow, put the open triangle of one parallelogram into the triangular pocket of another. Work clockwise in the same way to complete a circle. Use tape to secure your Trusty Rainbow together on the back side. Now try tossing your Trusty Rainbows to family members and friends!

Pressed Rainbows

Simple Supplies: You'll need masking tape, small paper clips, rainbow colors of Plasticine or Fimo clay (available at craft stores), and two 3-inch squares of clear Plexiglas for each person. Be sure the Plexiglas is 1/16-inch thick. Plexiglas is found at glass and window stores and can be easily cut with X-Acto knives.

Directions: Explain to families that they'll be making beautiful sun-catchers as reminders of the story of Noah and his trust in God. Several pairs of hands are needed at various times throughout the creation of these unique window rainbows, so encourage families to work closely together.

Hand each person two squares of Plexiglas. Demonstrate how to place tiny balls and strips of clay on the square of Plexiglas to make rainbow shapes or random designs. Gently place the second piece of Plexiglas on top of the clay design, then press gently down on this piece of Plexiglas and watch the clay squish and blend together in beautiful swirls and colors!

When your Pressed Rainbow is exactly as you want it, hold the square while another person carefully tapes along the edges to create a frame. Tape small paper clips to the Plexiglas as hangers.

Have families take their projects home to hang in windows where they can trust God to send the sunshine to make them gleam!

FESTIVAL FOOD

Rainbow Roll-Ups

Simple Supplies: You'll need flour tortillas, colored sugar or multicolored cake decorating sprinkles, butter or margarine, plastic knives, paper plates and cups, and milk or fruit juice.

Directions: These yummy rainbows are a delightful springtime treat!

Encourage people to wash their hands, then distribute a flour tortilla to each person. Spread an even layer of butter or margarine on one side of the tortilla. Gently sprinkle on a generous amount of colored sugar or candy sprinkles. Then roll the tortilla into a tube. Eat the treat as a tube or cut it into slices. Inside you'll discover a beautiful sparkly rainbow!

While families enjoy these bite-sized rainbows with glasses of milk or fruit juice, encourage them to talk about the seasons and what they can trust God to provide in each.

FESTIVAL FINALE

Trust in God

Simple Supplies: You'll need Bibles, pens, and the Trusty Rainbows made in the Festival Crafts section.

Have families open their Bibles to Genesis 9:7-17 and follow along as a volunteer reads the passage aloud. Ask everyone to point out ways Noah trusted God. Challenge families to discuss areas of their lives they can trust God to help with, such as school, family relationships, or their health. Write ways we can trust God on the Trusty Rainbows.

Close with individual family prayers referring to the Trusty Rainbows to thank God for ways they trust him. Encourage families to ask God's help in developing more trust in him.

Rainbow Seeds

Simple Supplies: *You'll need small resealable plastic bags, multicolored cake decorating sprinkles, a stapler, and copies of the Rainbow Seeds poem below.*

As families are leaving the Colors of Spring Fling, have them each take a sandwich bag of candy sprinkles with the Rainbow Seeds poem stapled to it. Encourage family members to give the Rainbow Seeds to someone to remind that person of Noah, his trust in God, and the promise of God's rainbow.

Rainbow Seeds

It's a stormy, gloomy, grumpy day.
Everybody's in your way.
Do you think Noah had a day like this
When everything seemed all amiss?

God put a rainbow in the sky,
His promise to Noah—way up high!
Now you can have a rainbow too.
To remind you to trust God's promises too.

Just sprinkle these RAINBOW SEEDS around,
And God's promise of love will surely abound.
God's love will help you smile and grin—
And a happy day can then begin!

Planting Instructions

Sprinkle RAINBOW SEEDS in or on:
❀ your morning cereal
❀ your toothpaste
❀ a sandwich
❀ a glass of milk
❀ your tongue, for kinder words

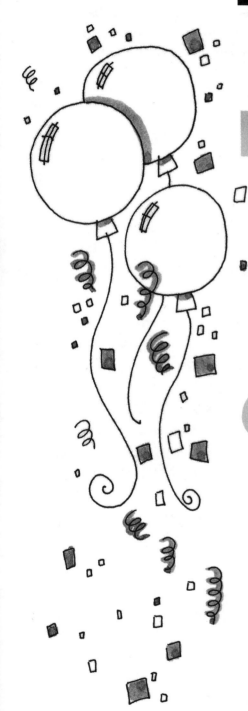

**Family
Faith Builder:**

Joy

EASTER EXTRAVAGANZA

Celebrate the joy of Jesus in this special family "eggstravaganza"!

BIBLE BASIS: Matthew 28:1-8

Easter is a celebration of great joy for Christians. After all, it's the climax of our beliefs in the deity of Jesus, in our salvation, and in the eternal life God's Son offers us. However, celebrating the joyful resurrection of Jesus can get lost in plastic eggs, chocolate bunnies, and jelly beans. How about turning these Easter distractions into powerful reminders of Jesus' resurrection and new life? Invite families to the Easter Extravaganza on Easter Sunday or in the days immediately following to celebrate the joy of Jesus' resurrection and new life.

GETTING READY

Each activity in this family festival contains its own list of simple supplies. Simply choose and use the activities that fit your needs and time requirements, then gather the appropriate supplies. Use one or more of these decorating and invitation suggestions to enliven your special event:

★ Build excitement for your Easter Extravaganza with an "invitational" egg hunt. Hide plastic pull-apart eggs throughout the church and church yard. Include details about the extravaganza on photocopied invitations inside the eggs.

★ Give each child or family a plastic Easter egg to decorate (or let them use the eggs they found in the invitational egg hunt). Encourage

Festival Finesse

As the families arrive, hand each person a plastic egg with one jelly bean (red, yellow or green) inside. This egg will be used throughout the entire festival.

families to bring their decorated eggs to the festival to use for activities or decorations.

★ Decorate the festival area with pastel paper streamers. Suspend plastic eggs from yarn or fishing line from the ceiling and doorways.

★ Festive favors and prizes might include small crosses, silk Easter lilies, and tiny baskets with Scripture verses inside.

FESTIVAL GAMES

Roll-Away Race

Simple Supplies: You'll need plastic Easter eggs, jelly beans, and chairs. Put a jelly bean in each egg and prepare one egg for every family. If you distributed eggs and jelly beans at the start of the festival, use these for this game.

Directions: Before beginning this rollicking race, ask families to name something that was rolled away on the first Easter morning. Then tell families that this lively race will remind them how the angel rolled away the stone from Jesus' tomb on that joyous Easter morning.

Form family lines at one end of the playing area. Place a chair about 6 feet away from each line. Hand the first person in each line a plastic egg with a jelly bean inside. Explain that the first person in line may choose one way to roll her egg around the chair and back. Ways to roll the eggs might include with feet, fingers, noses, or while walking backward. Tell everyone to get ready for some unexpected fun as the jelly beans make the eggs roll in humorous ways! When the first player returns to the line, the next player chooses a new way to roll her egg. As families finish the race, have them shout, "The stone's been rolled away, and Jesus is alive today!"

Joyful, Joyful, Jelly Bean!

Simple Supplies: You'll need a plastic egg and a red, yellow, or green (or any three colors you choose) jelly bean for each person. If you distributed eggs and jelly beans at the start of the festival, use them for this game.

Directions: Jump right up and jog for joy in this lively game as you celebrate the joy Mary must have experienced that first Easter morning. Remind families of the joy Mary felt as she excitedly ran to tell the disciples that Jesus was alive!

Have participants sit in a circle and choose a volunteer to be Mary. Be sure everyone has an egg with a jelly bean inside. Play this game as you would the age old favorite, Duck, Duck, Goose, but have Mary tiptoe from person to person saying, "Joyful, Joyful, Jelly Bean!" as she touches their heads. As Mary taps someone and says, "Jelly bean," both players open their plastic eggs. If their jelly beans are the same color, Mary tries to jog around the circle with the player in pursuit. If Mary gets to the place in the circle and sits down without getting tagged, the other player becomes the next Mary. If Mary is tagged, she takes another turn. If the jelly beans don't match, Mary keeps tapping heads until a match is made.

Play until everyone has had a turn to be Mary or a chaser. You'll want everyone to experience a little Easter joy by jogging around the circle!

Festival Finesse

Remind families that the colorful jelly beans we munch at Easter time symbolize the stone the angel rolled from Jesus' tomb, while the bright colors express the joy we feel knowing that Jesus is alive!

FESTIVAL CRAFTS

Beanie Tambourines

Simple Supplies: You'll need 7-inch clear plastic plates (available at party stores), staplers, permanent markers, clear packing tape, and jelly beans. (You may want to use the leftover jelly bean colors from the Festival Finale.) Be sure you have two 7-inch plastic plates and at least eight jelly beans for each person.

Directions: Use these creative tambourines while singing the happy and joyful music of Easter. Is your group ready to show off their new Easter percussion ensemble?

Give two clear plastic plates to each person. Use markers to decorate the bottom inside portion of one plate with an Easter scene. Pictures might include the empty tomb, angels, or bright sunshine. If you wish, have young children wear paint shirts to cover their clothing.

When the pictures are finished, have an adult staple the two plates together, leaving a small opening to poke in eight to ten jelly beans that will create the noise-making fun of a tambourine. Point out that the jelly beans are held inside the plates but that the tomb couldn't hold Jesus—he triumphed over death and is alive! Place a bit of tape over the staples so they don't scratch or catch on clothing.

Sing an Easter song of your choosing or use the one below, sung to the tune of "Mary Had a Little Lamb." Joyfully shake, rattle, and roll your Beanie Tambourines along with the beat!

Mary had a story to tell,	She ran and gave a shout of joy,
story to tell, story to tell.	Shout of joy, shout of joy.
Mary had a story to tell,	She ran and gave a shout of joy,
That Jesus is alive!	That Jesus is alive!

Jolly Egg-Heads

Simple Supplies: You'll need scissors, potting soil, grass seed, spoons, water, markers, empty egg cartons with the cups cut apart, and a plastic pull-apart egg for each person.

Directions: Gather families and explain that the egg is a symbol of new life. Remind them that Jesus offers us new life when we love him and accept him as our Savior. And what better way to celebrate the promise of new life in Jesus than by making these Jolly Egg-Heads?

Hand each person a plastic egg and an egg cup. Use permanent markers to draw funny faces on one side of each egg. You may also want to decorate the egg carton cups. Open the eggs and use spoons to fill the bottom halves of the eggs with soil. Plant the grass seeds according to the package instructions. Gently water the soil, making sure not to over-water, then replace the other half of the egg. Tell families to set their Jolly Egg-Heads in sunny spots. These little greenhouses will help the seeds sprout in 3 to 4 days. When the seeds have sprouted, remove the top half of each egg to let the sun shine in! After the grass seed has grown, style your Egg-Head's "hair" into ponytails, buzz cuts, or even braids. Remember to water the miniature gardens when they seem dry.

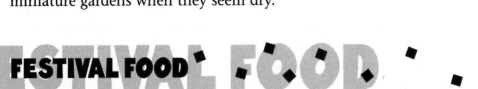

Jolly Bean Butterflies

Simple Supplies: You'll need access to an oven, damp cloths, pretzel sticks, and the following items for every ten people: a can of refrigerator biscuits, five plastic Easter eggs, assorted colors of tiny jelly beans, and a nonstick baking sheet.

Directions: Explain to participants that the butterfly is a wonderful Easter symbol of new life. Point out how the butterfly begins in a cocoon as a caterpillar, then emerges with new life as a butterfly. Remind everyone that Jesus' lifeless body was laid in the tomb but that he emerged with new life in the resurrection on Easter morning. Explain that families will be making butterfly treats to remind everyone of the joy of Jesus' victory over death.

Have people wash their hands and wipe off their work area. To make each butterfly, flatten one refrigerator biscuit. Using half of a plastic Easter egg as a biscuit cutter, press down in the center of the biscuit to create a dough circle and an outer ring. Gently pick up the outer ring and give it one twist to make the body of a butterfly. Gently pinch the dough circle to make wings, then place the body twist on the pinched area. Decorate the wings with brightly colored jelly beans. Add pretzel sticks as antennas.

Carefully place the butterfly biscuits on nonstick baking sheets and bake them in a 350 degree oven for about 10 minutes or until light brown.

As you're eating your Jolly Bean Butterflies, have families discuss questions such as "What are some of the joyful changes that Jesus has brought into your life?" and "How do we let others know about the new life they can have through Jesus?"

You've "Bean" There!

Simple Supplies: You'll need a Bible, several bags of mixed colors of jelly beans, three bowls, and plastic Easter eggs.

Empty the jelly beans into the three bowls. Be sure each person has a plastic Easter egg. Then have participants sit on the floor in three groups. Set the large bowls of jelly beans in the center of each group. Explain that you'll use jelly beans and their colors to tell the Easter story. When you indicate, people are to place the appropriate-colored jelly beans in their eggs.

Say: **Imagine that you've "bean" there—you saw the first joyful Easter! At the orange dawn on the first day of the week, Mary Magdalene and the other Mary went to visit Jesus' tomb. Place an orange jelly bean in your egg to remind you of the sunrise. Pause. There was a violent earthquake and an angel of the Lord came down from heaven and rolled back the stone in front of the tomb. Place a black jelly bean in your egg to remind you of the stone the angel rolled away. Pause.**

Festival Finesse

Have families write "Matthew 28:1-8" on their eggs with permanent markers. Be sure to have festival-goers take their Easter story eggs home!

The angel was bright as lightning, and his clothes were white as snow. Place a white jelly bean in your plastic egg to remind you of the angel. Pause. The angel told the women, "Don't be afraid—I know you're looking for Jesus, who was crucified." Place a red jelly bean in your egg to remind you of Jesus' shed blood on the cross. Pause. Then the angel said, "He is not here; he has risen! Go quickly and tell his disciples. Jesus is alive!" Place a purple jelly bean in your egg to remind you of Jesus, the risen king! Pause.

The women hurried away to tell the others the joyous news. Jesus is alive forever! Place a green jelly bean in your egg to remind you of the new life on that first Easter.

Encourage families to use their story eggs to retell the joyous Easter story at home.

Pray for Albania Club

Bring the hope, joy, and new life Jesus offers to a country where parents were recently forbidden to teach children about Jesus. Begin your own Pray for Albania Club so that more people in this country may learn about the joy and new life Jesus Christ offers. Read about Albania, then meet with your club on a regular basis to pray for the people. To see how your family can help send Bibles and Christian newspapers and books to Albania, write to:

Youth With a Mission
P.O. Box 55309
Seattle, WA 98155

WEATHER WONDERS

Calm "stormy seas" on a rainy afternoon with Jesus' miracles.

BIBLE BASIS: Luke 8:22-25

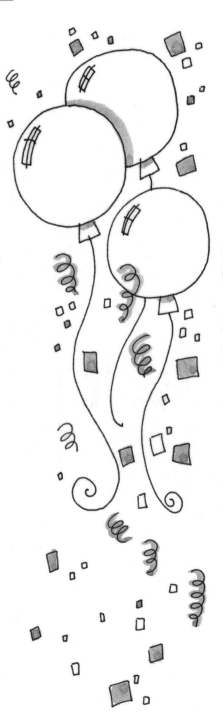

April showers bring May flowers, but they also bring frightening lightning and rumbling thunder. A violent spring storm can cause just about anyone to be afraid. Jesus' disciples didn't feel very courageous when stranded in the middle of a stormy sea. But Jesus was with them and miraculously calmed the storm and their fears. Families need to remember that Jesus is with them when they weather the storms in their lives too. So muster up a bit of courage and celebrate a stormy afternoon with this Weather Wonders celebration during the month of April—or anytime you need a calming dose of courage!

GETTING READY

Each activity in this family festival contains its own list of simple supplies. Simply choose and use the activities that fit your needs and time requirements, then gather the appropriate supplies. Use one or more of these decorating and invitation suggestions to enliven your special event:

★ Photocopy invitation information for the Stormy Weather Wonders celebration on blue paper, then cut individual invitations into raindrops.

★ Advertise this festival at church by handing out invitations while wearing a raincoat and boots. Don't forget an umbrella!

★ Use yellow crepe paper to make bright suns on the walls and the door of the room where your festival will take place. Wind the crepe paper in spiral circles, creating the sun's rays with 2-to-3-foot lengths of crepe paper coming out from the sides.

★ Suspend paper raindrops from real umbrellas that you've hung from ceilings and doorways. Scatter paper raindrops on tables and around the floor.

★ Festival favors and prizes might include paper beverage umbrellas, small toy boats, sponges, watercolor paints, or sunny yellow butterscotch discs!

FESTIVAL GAMES

Bail Out!

Simple Supplies: You'll need cereal-sized paper or Styrofoam bowls, water, two large buckets, and paper cups.

Directions: Tell families that they may need to have a bit of courage for this "sea-worthy" game! Play outside or in a place where everyone can get a little damp. (If you prefer, use popped popcorn instead of water.)

Form family boat crews and have them stand at one end of the playing area. Place a water-filled bucket by the boat crews and an empty bucket about 15 feet away. Hand children paper bowls to hold on their heads as boats. Hand adults paper cups and tell them that they are the storm-dippers.

Explain that in this fast-paced game, the storm-dippers will use paper cups to pour water into the boats. Then the boats must "cross the sea" to the bucket on the opposite shore. Some boats may have a little more courage than others, while some may encounter more storms!

When they reach the shore, the boats must carefully bail the water (with the bowls still on their heads!) into the bucket, then rush back to the starting line for another fill-up. Play until all the water is in the bucket on the other shore. Count the number of trips each boat crew makes before the bucket is empty. Reward the courage of the crew with the most trips with construction paper "purple umbrellas of courage" if you'd like!

Festival Finesse

Try punching holes in the rims of the bowls and threading yarn through them. Tie the yarn under players chins, then…
"Anchors away!"

Going Down

Simple Supplies: You'll need one chair for every player except the captain.

Directions: Explain that this wild and rowdy Bible-based game may just be what you need to burn off that extra energy on a stormy day.

Arrange the chairs in a large circle boat, then encourage everyone to find a seat. As the leader of the festival, you can be the boat's captain for the first round. The captain stands in the center of the circle and says, "We're going down, but will we drown?" as many times as she likes. The players stay seated until the captain adds the phrase, "Where is your faith?" At these words, the seated players and the captain jump up and say, "My faith's in Jesus!" and then rush to switch seats. Encourage crew members to move across the circle and not merely exchange seats with a neighbor! The player without a seat in the boat becomes the new captain.

Encourage the boat captain to speed up her phrases or to add other phrases such as "Who do we trust?" or "Who can save us?" All the players will need to listen carefully, or the overeager player may lose his seat to the wily captain!

When the game comes to an end, encourage family members to talk about times they needed to have courage because they thought they were going to "drown" in some area of their life and about how Jesus helped them.

FESTIVAL CRAFTS

Rain Stick

Simple Supplies: You'll need popcorn kernels, uncooked rice, masking tape, and markers (or patterned Con-Tact paper). You'll also need a half sheet of paper and a cardboard tube for each Rain Stick.

Directions: Create these awesome musical Rain Sticks on a stormy day even if you're getting tired of the sound of rain.

For each Rain Stick, cover one end of a cardboard tube with masking tape. Sprinkle about 1 tablespoon each of popcorn kernels and uncooked rice kernels into the tube. Tear the half sheet of paper into six squares—don't worry about their exact size! Gently crumple these squares and place them inside the tube. These will help funnel the kernels through the tube to create a more authentic sound of falling rain. Seal off the open end of the tube with masking tape.

Invite families to decorate their Rain Sticks with markers or cover them with patterned Con-Tact paper. Now gently tip the Rain Sticks from side to side to hear the soothing sounds of gentle rain. After you're done playing with the Rain Sticks, set them aside to be used during the Festival Finale.

Windometer

Simple Supplies: You'll need markers and colored tape (optional). You'll also need a 9-inch length of 3/4-inch dowel and a 2-by-45-inch strip of wind cloth such as Rip-Stop or nylon (available at any fabric store) for each Windometer.

Directions: Remind participants that when Jesus calmed the stormy sea, wind nearly capsized the boat, but when Jesus spoke to the wind and commanded it to stop, it did! Explain that you'll make Windometers to measure the wind and remind everyone that Jesus controls even the wind and rain.

Give each person a dowel to decorate with markers. When the dowels are decorated, give each person a 45-inch length of wind cloth to tie or tape securely to one end of the dowel. If the weather permits, have people go outside and stand some distance from each other while they hold their Windometers with outstretched arms. Observe which way the wind is blowing, then try running against the wind to see what happens to the Windometers. If there is no wind, instruct people to run and watch what happens to their Windometers.

When you finish checking out the wind, set the Windometers aside to be used during the Festival Finale. Tell families that when they take their projects home, they can hang their Windometers on porches or patios.

FESTIVAL FOOD

Seaside Sandwiches
Simple Supplies: You'll need quart-sized resealable plastic bags, graham crackers, powdered blueberry gelatin mix, nondairy whipped topping, candy gummy fish, measuring spoons and cups, napkins, and paper plates.

Directions: You'll never guess what washed up on shore after a storm—it never tasted so good! And it doesn't take much courage to eat this yummy snack.

Give each person a resealable plastic bag. Have participants open the bags and measure in 1/2 cup nondairy whipped topping, 1/4 teaspoon blueberry gelatin powder, and several gummy fish. Reseal the bags, then gently cause a few waves, mixing the gelatin powder into the whipped topping.

Make tasty "seashores" by placing graham crackers on paper plates, then opening the plastic bags and squeezing the contents onto the crackers. Just look what washed up on shore!

FESTIVAL FINALE

Row, Row, Row Your Boat
Simple Supplies: You'll need Bibles, newsprint, a marker, and the Rain Sticks and Windometers made during craft time.

Copy the words to the song in this activity on a sheet of newsprint and hang it on a wall for everyone to see (or project it on a screen).

Invite family groups to find places to sit together, open their Bibles to Luke 8:22-25, and follow along as a volunteer reads the passage aloud. Then have family groups discuss these questions:

★ How are courage and faith related? How can Jesus help us have both?

★ When are times you've felt alone and like you're rowing a boat on stormy seas? How did Jesus help you?

★ Who is someone our family could help become more courageous and faith-filled?

In closing, lead families in singing the following song to the tune of "Row, Row, Row Your Boat." Use the Rain Sticks and Windometers to make accompanying motions and sound effects. When you're familiar with the words and motions, try singing the song in a round.

Row, row, row your boat *(Use Windometers as oars.)*
On the stormy sea. *(Wave the Windometers over the floor.)*
Wind may blow and rain flow, *(Wave Windometers and shake Rain Sticks.)*
But faith can set us free! *(Wildly shake Rain Sticks.)*

FAMILY FESTIVAL FOLLOW-UP

Stormy Weather Helpers

Extend your Weather Wonders festival by taking note of areas hard hit by spring weather. Each year different areas in the United States are hit by floods, tornadoes, and hurricanes. Contact your local American Red Cross or even the National Chapter (1-800-417-0495) to see how your family can help others in need. The Red Cross is always looking for courageous workers to provide resources for people devastated by stormy weather.

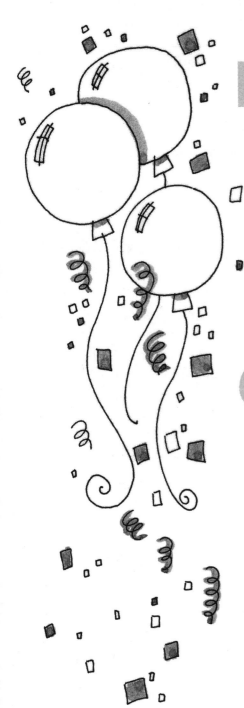

**Family
Faith Builder:**

Prayer

DEAR GOD . . .

Commemorate the National Day of Prayer with this meaningful family festival.

BIBLE BASIS: Matthew 6:9-15

The National Day of Prayer, celebrated on the first Thursday of May, is a time for Christians everywhere to stop, open their hearts, and pray to God. Prayers for family members, friends, governments, and countries are lifted up together at noon on that powerful day. And God hears every prayer! What a wonderful commemoration for an activity that should take place in our lives every day. Join together on the evening before the National Day of Prayer to discover Jesus' perfect prayer and to prepare your hearts and minds for the meaningful day to follow.

GETTING READY

Each activity in this family festival contains its own list of simple supplies. Simply choose and use the activities that fit your needs and time requirements, then gather the appropriate supplies. Use one or more of these decorating and invitation suggestions to enliven your special event:

★ Invitations can be copied on the backs of National Day of Prayer flyers, which you can create to advertise the holiday. Or make copies of flyers distributed by other churches in your community. Be sure to distribute flyers advertising your festival throughout the neighborhoods surrounding your church about a week before the festival.

★ This is a wonderful festival to hold in the evening. Light candles or use electric candles or Christmas tree lights. Dim the lights to create a prayerful mood.

★ Flags from others countries make a nice backdrop for doors and walls and encourage families to pray for others in the world.

★ Party prizes and favors could include small crosses, special candles, praying hands bookmarks, and colorful notepads to keep records of prayers.

FESTIVAL GAMES

P. D. S. (Prayer Delivery Service)

Simple Supplies: You'll need large marshmallows, plastic spoons, fine-tipped markers, and masking tape.

Directions: Before the festival, place masking tape start and finish lines 12 feet apart in the playing area.

Gather families and point out that prayer reaches God without postal systems or telephone lines. He hears every prayer if we just talk to him.

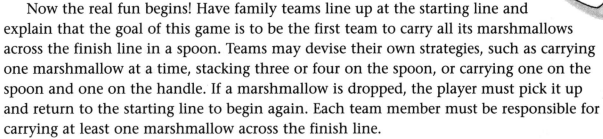

Form family groups and give each group a plastic spoon, ten large marshmallows, and a marker. Have the groups discuss prayers they need in the coming week. Prayers could be for a big math test, a birthday celebration, a small child just learning to walk, or a sick pet. Using the markers, write a key word for each of these requests on the large marshmallows.

Now the real fun begins! Have family teams line up at the starting line and explain that the goal of this game is to be the first team to carry all its marshmallows across the finish line in a spoon. Teams may devise their own strategies, such as carrying one marshmallow at a time, stacking three or four on the spoon, or carrying one on the spoon and one on the handle. If a marshmallow is dropped, the player must pick it up and return to the starting line to begin again. Each team member must be responsible for carrying at least one marshmallow across the finish line.

When a family's marshmallows are "home," have the family shout, "Teamwork works!" Then have everyone find a place to sit down and remind families that praying together is teamwork. Point out that no prayer is too big or too small for God to hear or answer. God hears every prayer. Encourage families to pray for the requests written on the marshmallows during the coming week.

Concentrate on Prayer

Simple Supplies: No supplies required.

Directions: Form two groups of families and choose one person to be the statue. Have the remaining players be prayer partners and sit in a circle around the statue. Challenge the prayer partners to carefully study the statue for a several moments. Then have the statue walk out of the room and change something about her appearance. While the statue is gone, the prayer partners pray for her in general terms. When the statue returns, have prayer partners determine what has changed, such as a missing shoe or a wristwatch on the other arm. Whoever guesses correctly becomes the next statue.

After the game, gather everyone and explain that many things may change a person besides his outward appearance. Remind families that prayer changes people on the inside! Encourage families to pray for each other at least once this week.

FESTIVAL CRAFTS

Prayer Cards

Simple Supplies: You'll need Styrofoam plates, ballpoint pens, crayons, and 3-by-5-inch pieces of copy paper.

Directions: Remind families that God wants us to talk to him through prayer. Tell them that they'll be making Prayer Cards to let others know they're praying for them.

Give everyone a Styrofoam plate and a ballpoint pen. Invite participants to use the ballpoint pens to draw pictures and designs on the bottoms of the plates. Press the pens deeply enough to make indentations but not deeply enough to cut through the plates.

Once the drawings are etched into the plates, place squares of paper over the designs and use crayons to color over the paper. The design will appear on the paper and turn it into a lovely card. Have everyone turn the card over and write "(Name), I'm praying for you!" Have participants write the names of people they can pray for in the blank spaces and then sign their own names. Invite people to write additional notes on the backs of the Prayer Cards. Encourage everyone to make at least three cards, exchanging designs with other family members.

When the cards are complete, have families take them home to put in envelopes and mail to the appropriate people to let them know others are praying for them.

Hope and Pray Plants

Simple Supplies: You'll need bean sprout seeds (available in food stores), resealable sandwich bags, paper towels, markers, and spray bottles with water.

Directions: Tell families that each year as farmers around the world plant their crops, they pray that God will provide the sun and rain to help them grow. Remind everyone that God hears our prayers and answers them in his time and in his way. Explain that they'll be making little gardens to remind them to pray for world hunger.

Give each family member a resealable sandwich bag and a paper towel. Spray the paper towels with water to moisten them, then slide the towels into the plastic bags. Let participants sprinkle the seeds on the moist towels, then blow gently into the bags before sealing them tightly. Be sure to have each person write her initials on the bag.

Have families take their Hope and Pray Plant seeds home to tape to sunny windows. Encourage families to pray for the people in the world who grow the food we eat each time they see their Hope and Pray Plants. Watch the beans sprout and, after about a week, rinse them and put them in a tossed salad to eat and enjoy!

FESTIVAL FOOD

Prayer Peaches

Simple Supplies: *You'll need canned peach halves, graham crackers, marshmallow creme, plastic spoons and knives, cake sprinkles, and paper plates.*

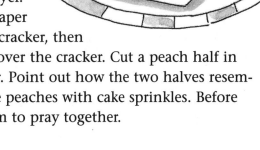

Directions: Explain that when we pray, we're looking to God for loving help, hope, and happiness. Remind everyone that it's important to look to God each day through quiet prayer. Tell families that this yummy snack will remind them to look to God through prayer.

Have each person place a graham cracker on a paper plate. Spoon marshmallow creme onto the graham cracker, then use the back side of the spoon to spread the creme over the cracker. Cut a peach half in two and place the halves side by side on the cracker. Point out how the two halves resemble two praying hands. For a colorful touch, top the peaches with cake sprinkles. Before families enjoy eating this fun snack, encourage them to pray together.

FESTIVAL FINALE

The Lord's Prayer

Simple Supplies: *You'll need Bibles.*

Invite families to find quiet places to sit. Have families open their Bibles to Matthew 6:9-15 and follow along as a volunteer reads the passage aloud. Ask people to point out the portions of the Lord's Prayer that could also be included in their daily prayers to God.

Then challenge family groups to discuss these questions:

★ When has prayer worked in your life or in the lives of others?

★ How has God answered a prayer differently than you expected? Why can we trust God's answers?

★ In what ways can praying for others help them? help us?

★ What is a prayer that you'd like answered in your life right now?

Explain to families that they can begin a prayer journal at home. Set a spiral notebook in a prominent place where all family members have

Festival Finesse

The acronym ACTS is a good way to remember the sections of the Lord's Prayer. A is for adoration. C is for confession. T is for thanksgiving. S is for supplication.

access to it. When a member of the family has or knows of a prayer concern, write it in the prayer journal. Family members should make a habit of checking the prayer journal and praying for the requests listed daily. Make a notation of answered prayer by each of the prayer requests in the journal to see how and when God answers prayers.

FAMILY FESTIVAL FOLLOW-UP

National Day of Prayer

Participate in or organize a prayer meeting for the National Day of Prayer in your church or community. Be sure to distribute flyers about the event, if it is not already being done in your community. Meet at noon to pray together in a designated place, such as a church yard or a park. Isn't it wonderful that you can know that on the first Thursday of May, people all over are joined together in prayer and in God's love?

MOTHER'S DAY TEA

Encourage Mom to relax during this festival centered around motherhood.

BIBLE BASIS: Exodus 2:1-10

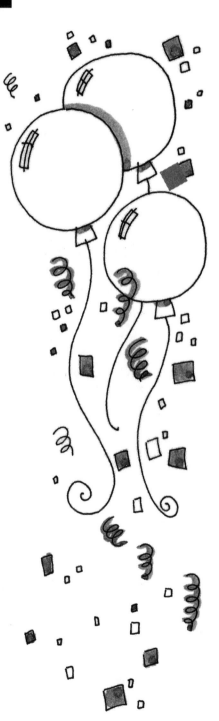

Motherhood is a tough job with no prior training. It's a job that requires loving commitment for her family in all that she does. Mothers mentioned in the Bible are few and far between. We know about Hannah's sacrificial love for Samuel, of Mary and Elizabeth's unquestioning faith in their sons, and of Ruth's son, Obed. But Moses' mother, who is not even named in the Exodus 2 account of his childhood, was the epitome of a loving, caring, and protective mother. Families will love celebrating their own special moms and other loving women in their lives with this special festival.

GETTING READY

Each activity in this family festival contains its own list of simple supplies. Simply choose and use the activities that fit your needs and time requirements, then gather the appropriate supplies. Use one or more of these decorating and invitation suggestions to enliven your special event:

★ Create unusual invitations to your Mother's Day Tea by attaching pretty note cards to tea bags.

★ Make this special event commemorating Moses' mother and all women beautiful by focusing on a water theme. Cover tables with white tablecloths, then create the Nile river down the center of each table by making a table runner from blue plastic wrap or wrapping paper.

★ Place clear glass bowls partially filled with water along the

Nile. Float flowers, flower petals, or floating candles on the surface. You may even want to add a few drops of blue food coloring to the water for a colorful touch.

★ Hang blue crepe-paper streamers across the ceiling or from light fixture to light fixture. Place streamers close together in a wave-like pattern with twists and turns to create the effect of a cascading waterfall.

★ Festival favors could include silk flowers or real plants, coupons for donuts or quick meals out, hankies, and any heart-shaped items.

FESTIVAL GAMES

Remembering Mom

Simple Supplies: For each group of eight to ten people, you'll need fifteen to twenty items that mothers use to care for their families. Suggested items include a washcloth; a cotton-tipped swab; a bar of soap; any travel-sized containers of shampoo, powder, or toothpaste; a small book; a Sunday school lesson or devotional; a granola bar or other wrapped food items; a pencil; or a plastic bandage.

Directions: Tell families that, just as Moses' mother took care of him, moms take care of their families every day in so many ways. Have family members use their observation skills for this game and, when the festival is over, to remember to thank Mom for all that she does!

Set the items on the floor and have everyone choose one to hide behind his back. After each person has an item, go around the circle with each person giving one or two clues to describe the item. For example, if the item is a bandage, a child might say, "Mom uses this to help me when I'm hurt or skin my knee." If the item is a Bible or Sunday school devotion paper, an adult might say, "This reminds me of how Mom made sure we got to church each week." After each clue, let others try to guess the item. Score one point for each family who guesses an item correctly. Continue until each person has had a turn to give clues.

When the game is over, have family groups pray and thank God for the gift of mothers and other loving women they know.

Moses in the Basket

Simple Supplies: You'll need blindfolds, masking tape, markers, several large pieces of newsprint with a large basket drawn on each, index cards, scissors, and parenting or family magazines. Be sure you have a blindfold for each family or, if you're rotating activities, supply up to six blindfolds.

Directions: Tape the pieces of newsprint with the baskets drawn on them to a wall or a door so that all ages are able to reach them. Remind everyone that moms care for their families in many ways. Ask volunteers to tell ways that baby Moses' mother cared for him. Then tell families they'll play a game to remind them of how Moses' mother protected him by placing him in the basket boat.

Gather families and give each a magazine and enough index cards for each family member to have one. Instruct families to cut out pictures of babies and then tape them to index cards. If players choose, they can draw pictures of babies right on the cards. Then stick small rolled pieces of masking tape to the back side of each index card. While families are doing this, encourage them to discuss ways moms care for and love their families.

Designate a basket picture for each family, then have families form lines about 10 feet from their pictures. Have family members hold their prepared cards. Explain that this game is played like a Pin the Tail on the Donkey relay. The object is to get all the babies in the basket while blindfolded. Blindfold one member from each family and have her walk toward the basket as the other family members give helpful verbal directions such as "a little lower!" or "more to the right!"

When the first baby Moses is in the basket, blindfold the next member on the team. Continue until everyone on the team has had a turn, then give each other high fives and a cheer! Briefly discuss how well family members did at helping everyone get baby Moses in the basket. Point out that taking care of and protecting each other can be hard work!

FESTIVAL CRAFTS

Daughter of the Nile Bubble Bath

Simple Supplies: You'll need four large bowls, powdered bath beads (Calgon works well), powdered bubble bath (such as Mr. Bubble), powdered milk, flower-shaped cake sprinkles, resealable sandwich bags, and plastic spoons.

Directions: Remind families that Pharaoh's daughter bathed in the Nile River before finding baby Moses among the weeds. Explain that they'll make a craft project Mom can use to take special care of herself—and to feel like royalty!

Pour each of the ingredients into a separate bowl, then place several plastic spoons in each bowl. Hand a resealable plastic bag to each person. (Moms can also make these crafts to present to their mothers or other special women they know.) Instruct participants to measure 3 spoonfuls of powdered bath beads, 3 spoonfuls of bubble bath, and 2 spoonfuls of powdered milk into their bags. Then put 1 spoonful of the flower-shaped sprinkles into each bag. Close the bags tightly and gently shake to mix ingredients. You may wish to decorate the bags with stickers or glue pretty labels with the name of the bubble bath on the fronts of the bags. Perhaps Mom could share just a little Daughter of the Nile Bubble Bath with the family. Ahh, the Nile never smelled so wonderful!

Bitsy Baskets

Simple Supplies: You'll need plastic berry baskets and any combination of the following weavable supplies: thick yarn, thick twine, raffia, computer paper tear-strips, crepe paper, ribbon, lace trim, or pot holder loops.

Directions: Tell families that Moses' mother worked hard to made a waterproof basket for him. Point out that moms and other loving women in our lives work hard for us too. Explain that they'll have fun working on pretty baskets to hold plants for them to care for or give to Mom or Grandma for Mother's Day.

Let each person select a berry basket and any of the weavable supplies. Demonstrate how to weave the materials in and out of the sides of the berry baskets, creating a dense woven effect. There's no need to connect ends before starting a new piece—just begin a new piece in the same square as the last piece finished. This craft will take a while for some, but others who like the loosely woven effect will be finished in a few minutes. Each basket will turn out unique and beautiful.

Place a bag of the Daughter of the Nile Bubble Bath inside a Bitsy Basket for a special gift to present during the Festival Follow-Up.

FESTIVAL FOOD

Eat-'Em-Up Baskets

Simple Supplies: You'll need large serving spoons, crispy rice cereal, shredded coconut, corn syrup, brown sugar, peanut butter, gallon-sized resealable plastic bags, measuring cups, jelly beans or gummy bears, and paper plates. You'll also want damp paper towels.

Directions: Explain that these yummy treats will remind people of Moses' basket boat. Hand each family a large resealable plastic bag. Have families measure out and pour into their bags 2 spoonfuls of corn syrup, 2 spoonfuls of brown sugar, and 4 spoonfuls of peanut butter. Reseal the bags and have family members take turns squeezing the bags to combine the ingredients. Open the bags and add 1 cup of crispy rice cereal and 1/3 cup of shredded coconut. Close the bags and gently combine the ingredients until they are well coated.

Remove small portions of the dough and place them on each person's paper plate. Form the dough into basket shapes and place a jelly bean or gummy bear in each basket to remind you of the story of baby Moses and how his mother cared for him. Use the damp paper towels to clean everyone's hands. If you desire, serve your special moms a cup of lemon tea for an extra treat.

FESTIVAL FINALE

Taking Care of Each Other

Simple Supplies: *You'll need your Bibles.*

Invite family groups to find quiet places to sit together. Have families open their Bibles to Exodus 2:1-10 and follow along as a volunteer reads the passage aloud. Ask everyone to point out ways Moses' mother took care of him, worked for him, protected him, and loved him. Then challenge family groups to think about and discuss one or more of these questions:

★ In what ways do moms care for us? How is this like the ways God cares for us?

★ How can caring for others draw us closer to God? to our families?

★ What can you do this week to thank Mom, or someone else, for caring for you?

Then encourage families to use the answers from the questions in a prayer. Begin each line of the prayer in a way similar to the one written below.

Thank you for moms who care for us when... (families insert their answers).

Please help us say thank-you this week by... (families insert their responses).

Thank you for giving us people to love and care for us. Amen.

End with a warm hug for Mom and the entire family!

FAMILY FESTIVAL FOLLOW-UP

Tender Loving Care

Is there a care center near your church or home? Most care centers are filled with older moms and grandmoms. Have your family set a date to go and visit moms in the center. Take along the Bitsy Baskets and the Daughter of the Nile Bubble Bath beads for special treats. If women aren't able to use the bubble bath, use a pin to poke a few small holes in the plastic bag or place the contents in used dryer softener sheets tied with bows. Place them in dresser drawers as sachets. Check with the nursing staff as you arrive to visit with those moms who might have no friends or relatives close by.

**Family
Faith Builder:**

Forgiveness

DAD'S DAY

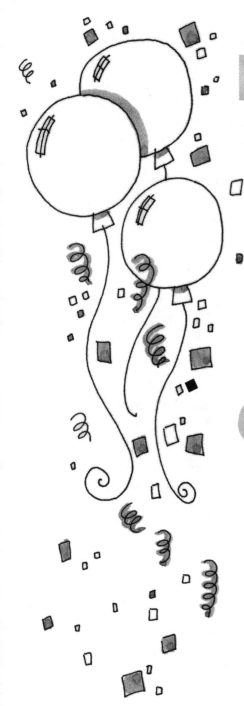

Celebrate God's forgiveness while honoring dads everywhere.

BIBLE BASIS: Luke 15:11-32

Most of us have had a father or father figure who served as a role model in our lives. It may have been our own loving father, a caring neighbor, or an adoring grandpa. But whoever this man was, he no doubt modeled goodness, forgiveness, and all we hoped to become in our own lives. Of course, our heavenly Father provides the perfect model of goodness and forgiveness, and the parable of the Prodigal Son reflects these values as a father's loving forgiveness helps a son who has done wrong. This earthly story with a heavenly meaning tells of God's loving forgiveness toward each of us. Celebrate Father's Day, our heavenly Father, and loving forgiveness with this fun, outdoor festival.

GETTING READY

Each activity in this family festival contains its own list of simple supplies. Simply choose and use the activities that fit your needs and time requirements, then gather the appropriate supplies. Use one or more of these decorating and invitation suggestions to enliven your special event:

★ For invitations, cut out pennant shapes from poster board and attach festival information on the back. Encourage families to decorate these family pennants with their names and bring them to the festival. Attach wooden dowels and poke the pennants into the ground around the area where your festival is being held.

Festival Finesse

Remind families that this festival is to honor dads or other loving men in their lives.

★ Begin or end the Dad's Day festival with a family picnic. Encourage families to pack their own picnic lunches to enjoy with other families at a nearby park or in your church's own backyard.

★ Plan on holding your entire festival outside, if weather permits. Decorate the area with brightly colored balloons and streamers strung from tree to tree. If it's a hot day, make sure you have plenty of water in coolers for thirsty families to drink.

★ Party prizes and favors might include small key chains, combs, or even funny neckties from a thrift store!

FESTIVAL GAMES

Big Burdens

Simple Supplies: *You'll need bricks, large stones, or books.*

Directions: Remind families that when they're unforgiving or when they're in need of forgiveness themselves, they carry a heavy burden. Explain that this game is about heavy burdens, so they'll need to loosen up their muscles for the fun in this game!

Pile the bricks, stones, or books in one area. Have each family member choose two items from the pile and find a place to stand. Explain that the object of this game is to hold the items, one in each hand, for the longest amount of time.

At a starting signal, have everyone hold a "heavy burden" in each hand as he stretches arms out to the sides. After several moments, begin talking about the weight of unforgiven sin and how heavy it feels. Explain that when burdens are too heavy to carry, we need to set down our burdens and ask forgiveness.

Continue talking until no one is left holding the items. Then have everyone get with a partner and tell how it felt to set down the loads. Challenge people to identify how this game was like being forgiven. Then have participants tell their partners about a time they needed forgiveness or a time they forgave someone and how it felt. Point out that when we're in need of forgiveness, God is always ready to forgive. We just need to ask.

You may want to award a brick or stone to each family. They will make great doorstops at home and be solid reminders of God's forgiveness.

Prodigal Parent

Simple Supplies: *You'll need a blindfold for each parent and the Mighty Megaphones created during the Festival Crafts section. If you choose not to make Mighty Megaphones, make paper ones from rolled newspaper, then secure the megaphones with tape.*

Directions: Make sure the playing area is level and free of dips, holes, or large rocks before beginning this game. Give each parent a blindfold and be sure everyone else has a megaphone. Briefly recount the story of the prodigal son. Then explain that the father of the prodigal son waited for his son to come home. Could he even have stood at the road calling for him? Play this fun, noisy game to call your parents home.

Have children help their parents put on blindfolds. Line the parents up side by side. Then have children hold their megaphones and stand in a line about 15 feet away from and facing the adults.

At a starting signal, encourage the kids to start calling for their parents. Have kids use their megaphones to make their voices loud so parents can hear them. Parents will need to walk slowly and sort out their own children's voices in the midst of all of the others. Parents who reach their children first are the winners. You may want to award throat lozenges or hard candies as humorous prizes!

End the game by using quiet voices to discuss why the man in the story wanted his son home and how forgiveness played a key role in making that happen. Briefly discuss how love and forgiveness are woven together and centered in God.

FESTIVAL CRAFTS

Mighty Megaphones

Simple Supplies: You'll need newspapers, markers, stickers, Bingo daubers, crayons, staplers or tape, and poster board cut into megaphone shapes. (See illustration.) You'll need one megaphone cutout for each person.

Directions: Is your church in a quiet neighborhood? Liven it up a bit with these roaring Mighty Megaphones.

Cover a table with newspapers and set out the craft materials. Distribute a poster-board megaphone shape to each person. Invite participants to use their creativity to decorate the shapes with the markers, crayons, stickers, or Bingo dauber dots. When one or both sides of the megaphone shapes are decorated, demonstrate how to roll the poster-board shapes into a cone and then staple or tape the edges to make a Mighty Megaphone.

Have families join together and encourage them to use the megaphones to make up short cheers that tell about their dads or other loving men they know. Cheers can be serious or humorous. For example, a family might cheer, "He's our dad, he's so rad—We love him so, through rain or snow!" or "D-A-D, can't you see? He's the best in our fam-i-ly!" Invite families to present their cheers for everyone, and encourage lively applause after each rousing cheer!

Forgiveness Fans

Simple Supplies: You'll need paper plates, wooden sticks used to stir paint (available free from paint stores), clear packing tape or staplers, and markers or crayons.

Directions: Point out that sometimes even the most loving families have arguments or get hot under the collar with each other. When that happens, we need to cool off and offer forgiveness to one another. Explain that making Forgiveness Fans will remind everyone to cool off and offer forgiveness—before tempers get too hot!

Hand a paper plate and paint-stirring stick to each person. Instruct participants to use markers or crayons to decorate both sides of the plates. Then tape or staple the paint sticks to the bottoms of the plates to make fans.

Dads need a bit of pampering, so encourage families to take a few moments to fan their dads. Then have families talk about how cool, refreshing air created by moving fans is like God's forgiveness. Point out that we can be refreshed when God forgives our sins. Say a family prayer thanking God for his loving forgiveness and for the love of your dad or other loving men you know.

 **FESTIVAL FOOD**

Simple S'mores

Simple Supplies: You'll need graham crackers, chocolate frosting, miniature marshmallows, plastic knives, paper plates and cups, lemonade, and plenty of washcloths or damp paper towels.

Directions: What a perfect outdoor treat for your outdoor event! Let Dad sit back and take a quick nap in the shade while you make an extra Simple S'mores just for him.

Give each person a paper plate and one large graham cracker with four sections. Don't forget to make an extra snack for Dad! Encourage everyone to break the graham cracker in half and spread frosting on one side of both halves. Stick several miniature marshmallows on one frosted cracker half before covering it with the other coated cracker. The frosting will keep the marshmallows inside your Simple S'mores. Now serve Dad his Simple S'mores with a cup of cool lemonade!

 **FESTIVAL FINALE**

Forgiving Each Other

Simple Supplies: You'll need Bibles, a large wastebasket, pencils, and paper.

Invite family groups to sit together and open their Bibles to Luke 15:11-32. Read along as families each take a turn reading a portion of the passage aloud. Then ask everyone to point out ways the father forgave his son and why. Challenge families to discuss one or more of these questions:

★ What do you find the most difficult to forgive in others?

★ How has your dad recently forgiven you?

★ In what ways is forgiveness an expression of love?

★ What specific action can you take this week to forgive someone?

Read aloud Psalm 103:12. Then invite each family member to take a piece of paper and pencil and write down one thing for which he needs to be forgiven. Then, as families pray for God's forgiveness, have each person think about the thing he listed. When the prayers are finished, crumple the papers and toss them into the wastebasket as a symbol of God's forgiveness and how that sin is forgotten.

FAMILY FESTIVAL FOLLOW-UP

Big Brothers/Big Sisters of America

Consider a one-to-one mentorship of a juvenile who is in need of a concerned adult. Mothers and fathers of teens over the age of eighteen can participate in this organization by committing to spend time each week with an at-risk child. Families can become involved in this organization by putting a portion of their weekly allowances, money spent on eating in restaurants, or money used to buy candy bars, pop, or popcorn at a movie into a designated container in their homes. When the container is full, donations can be made to the Big Brothers/Big Sisters group in your community or to the national headquarters at:

Big Brothers/Big Sisters of America
230 N. 13th Street
Philadelphia, PA 19107

HUG ME HOOPLA

A warm touch and a cooperative spirit are key ingredients in this hug-me-happy celebration.

BIBLE BASIS: Acts 2:42-47

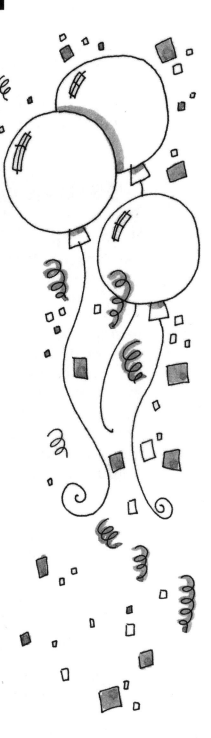

Cooperation is a value we want our children to learn early in life. It ranks right up there with sharing, saying thank-you, and loving our neighbors. Cooperation, sharing, and caring were evident in the lives of the early Christians mentioned in the book of Acts. They gave to people in need and helped each other spread the good news about Jesus. They shared meals and prayers. And they praised God together in all that they did. Use these early Christians as role models to help families learn the importance of cooperation and of growing nearer to God.

GETTING READY

Each activity in this family festival contains its own list of simple supplies. Simply choose and use the activities that fit your needs and time requirements, then gather the appropriate supplies. Use one or more of these decorating and invitation suggestions to enliven your special event:

★ Cut the fronts and backs off of empty cereal boxes or other boxed food products. Cut each section into three or four puzzle-shaped pieces. Photocopy and glue the festival information on the backs of these puzzle pieces. Be sure to include an appeal for each person to bring at least one canned food item for the food drive included in the Family Festival Follow-Up. Arrange extra puzzle pieces from the cereal boxes on the tables in your festival area, then encourage families to cooperate in putting these puzzles together as they arrive.

★ If possible, use the great outdoors for your festival. Set up one or two of the activities in the shade of a large tree or picnic shelter. You may even want to hold your festival in a nearby park, inviting park visitors to join in your celebration.

★ Create "Hug-Me-Hands" to use as decorations to hang from trees or tables or even to wrap around chair legs. Trace each of your hands on poster board, then tape a pipe cleaner between them. Twist, turn, and bounce your Hug-Me-Hands to display them all over your festival area.

★ Fill plastic or disposable latex gloves with air and tie them off with rubber bands. Place these "helping hands" throughout your festival area as a handy multipurpose decoration. At the end of the Hug-Me Hoopla, release the air from the gloves and fill them with water. Tie the gloves like balloons, then go outside and have a wet and wild time playing catch with the helping hands. What a fun way to cool off on a hot day!

★ Party favors might include gloves, plastic rings, or hand lotion.

FESTIVAL GAMES

Cooperation Creation

Simple Supplies: You'll need one or two large balls of yarn or string and several large cans of fruits or vegetables.

Directions: Remind families that Christian cooperation is very important, then ask participants to list ways Christians cooperate. Explain that in this game they will see how cooperation can create something beautiful.

Have families form a circle. If your group is very large, form circles with four families each. Tie the end of a ball of yarn around each can of food. Set a can in the middle of each circle to keep the end of the yarn in place. Begin by tossing the ball of yarn to someone in the circle, then have that person tell about a situation in which cooperation is essential, such as riding a tandem bicycle, playing a team sport, singing in the choir, or organizing a missions drive. Have this player hold the yarn and then toss it to another player. Continue tossing and holding the yarn and soon a lovely geometric pattern will appear in the center of the circle!

When everyone has tossed the ball of yarn at least once, hold the yarn and number off by twos around the circle. Have the number ones drop their yarn. Tell the number twos to cooperatively back up to pick up the slack. Point out that the pattern has changed and that it's now harder for those left in the circle to cooperate. Then have the number twos drop the yarn. Ask players what happens at church when people don't cooperate. Then ask what might happen if Christians didn't cooperate in getting the news about Jesus out to the world.

End by having families toss the ball of yarn in reverse order to wind it up. Cooperation is crucial or you may end up in knots!

Cooperation Dominoes

Simple Supplies: You'll need colored construction paper, pencils, scissors, masking tape, and a large room or play area.

Directions: This fun game can be played over and over again to form many different co-operative domino combinations. The more people who cooperate, the more fun it becomes.

Have each person trace around her hands on construction paper, then cut them out. Participants may choose to make both hand cutouts from the same color of paper or from different colors. When the hands are finished, have families tape the paper hands over each other's real hands. Explain that this game is played like dominoes, only people will match colors instead of dots. Encourage everyone to cooperate and communicate to figure out a way to have every player find a match.

Have families form two teams and stand at opposite ends of the room or playing area. Choose a person from one of the teams to stand in the center of the room and hold out his arms. Tell players to note the color of the paper hands. Then have someone from the other team who can match a color of either paper hand join hands with the first person. Continue taking turns until all of the hands are matched. Encourage teams to adopt a cooperative strategy to solve this fun puzzle!

When everyone is connected, move toward the center while still holding hands. Then end with a quick group hug.

FESTIVAL CRAFTS

Hug-Wraps

Simple Supplies: You'll need several large plastic coffee-can lids, pencils, scissors, colored embroidery floss or colored crochet thread, transparent tape, and matte board or very sturdy cardboard.

Directions: Gather families and explain that we cooperate with others in nearly everything we do. Ask for several examples, then explain that family members will need to cooperate with each other to finish these craft projects.

To make each Hug-Wrap, trace around a plastic coffee-can lid to create a large circle on matte board or sturdy cardboard. Cut out the paper circles. Young children may need extra help with this step if you're using matte board. Then cut six 1/2-inch slits around the edge of the circle. Space the slits about 2 inches apart.

Tape one end of the floss or thread to one side of the circle. Wind the embroidery floss or thread from slit to slit, around and around the other side of the circle. Try crisscrossing the floss from one side of the circle to another. Change colors of floss or thread by tying another color to the end and continuing to wind until you're satisfied with the colors and designs you chose.

As families work, point out how the floss wraps the circles like we wrap others in hugs. Encourage families to tell how a loving attitude makes cooperation easier and more productive.

When the Hug-Wraps are complete, cut the ends of the thread and tape them to the backs of the circles. Tie or tape a loop of thread to the top of each craft as a hanger, then invite families to hang their Hug-Wraps in windows or on walls for everyone to enjoy. Close by having family members give each other several hugs!

Scribble-n-Pass Place Mats

Simple Supplies: You'll need white paper place mats (available from restaurant supply stores or party goods stores), markers, and clear Con-Tact paper (optional).

Directions: These pretty place mats encourage creativity and teamwork. Plan on making extra place mats to include with your donation to a local food bank. (See Family Festival Follow-Up.)

Hand each family member a white paper place mat. Have family members sit in a circle. Give each family a set of markers. Have each family member draw a scribble or quick design on the place mat and then pass the place mat to the right so the next person can add to the drawing. Continue drawing and passing until the place mats end up in their original starting places.

Then ask families to choose a favorite Scripture verse about loving each other and to write that verse on their place mats. Good verses to include might be "Let us love one another, for love comes from God" (1 John 4:7) or "The man who loves God is known by God" (1 Corinthians 8:3). Finally, cover the place mats with clear Con-Tact paper to make them durable. It's fun to watch cooperative creativity in progress!

FESTIVAL FOOD

Hug-Me Bread

Simple Supplies: You'll need large mixing bowls, small bowls, flour, yeast, salt, sugar, softened butter, warm water, aluminum pie pans, measuring cups and spoons, nonstick cooking spray, medium-sized rubber bands, Hershey's chocolate candy Hugs or Kisses, and access to an oven.

Directions: Have family members pair up to create this special bread filled with love!

Have people form pairs or trios. Then tell everyone to rubber band one hand to one of her partner's hands and to place the other hand behind her back. Explain that partners will need to work cooperatively to make their goodies.

Have partners measure into a small bowl 2 tablespoons of yeast, 1 cup of warm water, and 1 tablespoon of softened butter. Let this mixture set while you mix together in a large bowl 1 1/2 cups of flour, 1 teaspoon of salt, and 1 tablespoon of sugar. Pour the yeast mixture into the large bowl with the flour mixture and stir to moisten the dough. Mix and knead the bread dough for 1 minute, then spray an aluminum pan with nonstick cooking spray.

Pat the bread into a flat, round loaf. Place the round dough into the pan. Unwrap several Hershey's Hugs or Kisses and place them on the loaf of bread. Gently pull and pinch the corners of the dough up and around the candies like a "sweet hug."

Place the dough in a 400-degree oven and bake about 20 minutes or until the loaves are lightly browned. (If you have time during your festival, let the dough rise for 15 minutes before baking.)

After cleanup and while the bread is baking or cooling, have everyone join in the Festival Finale. When you're ready to eat your Hug-Me Bread, encourage partners to sit down together, pray, then share their warm bread and a hug. Remind families that the early Christians broke bread together often as they lived and served God and each other.

FESTIVAL FINALE

Christian Cooperation
Simple Supplies: You'll need a Bible for each family.

Encourage family groups to sit together. Have a volunteer read Acts 2:42-47 aloud as families follow along in their Bibles. Ask the entire group to name the ways that early Christians co-operated with each other as they served God. Then have them compare and contrast cooperation in the church today. Finally, challenge family groups to discuss these questions:

★ In what ways does your family cooperate and support each other?

★ How does cooperating with and loving others show our love for God?

Encourage families to name times they need to cooperate with, love, and support each other during the coming week. Then offer a family prayer thanking God for each family member and the love he contributes to your family. End the festival with warm hugs, then share your delicious Hug-Me Bread snack.

FAMILY FESTIVAL FOLLOW-UP

We CAN Support Others!

Organize a cooperative canned food drive. Form family groups and give each a large decorated box in which to collect cans of food from neighbors and friends, making sure to let them know that their donations will be given to a local food bank. Thank them for their cooperation. When your donations are delivered, be sure to include some of your own hand-crafted Scribble-n-Pass Place Mats. (See Festival Crafts activity.)

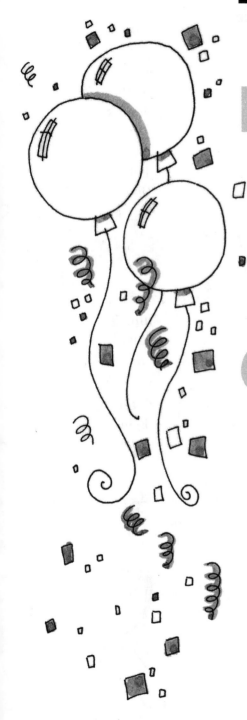

**Family
Faith Builder:**

Freedom

FREEDOM FESTIVAL

Celebrate our God-given blessing of freedom.

BIBLE BASIS: Joshua 1:1-9

Freedom. People have worked for it. People have fought for it. Yes, people have even died for it. Even the Israelites were willing to travel forty years for it. Why is freedom so important, and who can truly set us free? Learn more about freedom while discussing Joshua and the Israelites' taste of freedom as they entered the promised land. Celebrate freedom, a gift from God, in this fun, yet thought-provoking, family festival.

GETTING READY

Each activity in this family festival contains its own list of simple supplies. Simply choose and use the activities that fit your needs and time requirements, then gather the appropriate supplies. Use one or more of these decorating and invitation suggestions to enliven your special event:

★ Create a design-your-own-flag contest as a part of your festival invitations. Distribute large index cards with photocopied festival information taped to the back. Encourage families to design flags on the reverse sides of the cards. Make designs that could have symbolized the Israelites as they moved into the promised land. Or make family banner flags with your own family crest inventions. Encourage families to bring their completed entries to be displayed at the Freedom Festival.

★ Encourage festival-goers to wear red, white, or blue clothing or other colors representative of your country.

★ Decorate your festival room with flags, streamers, and balloons.

★ Party prizes and festival favors could include sparklers, banners, miniature flags, or colored caramel corn.

Freedom Ballooneyball

Simple Supplies: You'll need scissors, crepe paper, masking tape, and inflated red, white, and blue balloons.

Directions: Before beginning this game, hang several lengths of crepe paper across the middle of your playing area as a net. Tape or tie the crepe paper securely in place. Inflate several of each color balloon so you'll have one balloon for every two to three people.

Remind families that freedom is a gift from God, a gift that not all people are blessed with. To better understand this, play the following volleyball-type game.

Form three groups. Designate one group to hit only red balloons back and forth over the net. Have another group hit only the white balloons and a third group hit only the blue balloons back and forth over the net. Have group members stand on both sides of the net. Tell families that they'll volley the balloons back and forth but that any balloons that touch the ground will be removed from play. Explain that when you shout "Freedom!" players may hit any color balloon back and forth. But when you shout "Colors!" players must return to hitting only their specified colors.

Play for 5 minutes. The team with the most balloons at the end of the game wins. Have families give each other high fives. Then discuss some of the freedoms we may take for granted, such as free speech, freedom of religion, and our own salvation. Remind everyone that only God can give us true freedom!

Follow Joshua

Simple Supplies: No supplies required.

Directions: Tell families that they need to pretend they are the Israelites going into the promised land with Joshua as they play this version of the age-old favorite, Follow the Leader.

Designate one person in each family to be Joshua. Encourage Joshua to lead the Israelite followers through rooms in your church or outside while marching, whistling, flapping arms, or making other creative movements. Have families follow their Joshuas for about 60 seconds, then switch the role of Joshua to a different family member. When families end up in the festival room again, have them discuss ways Joshua and the Israelites may have celebrated their new freedom after they arrived in the promised land. Then briefly discuss how people celebrate freedom in your country.

Patriotic Poppers

Simple Supplies: You'll need 10-by-14-inch sheets of red, white, and blue wrapping paper (or other colors to represent your country). Patterned gift wrap works especially well!

Directions: Remind families that just as God's people fought to live in the promised land, their freedom was paid for through many battles and wars. Remind families that God was with the Israelites in battle and that God is with us too. Tell families that they'll make Patriotic Poppers to remember those who have fought in freedom battles.

Give one piece of paper to each person. (Younger children may want to make a Patriotic Popper with Mom or Dad at first.) Fold the paper lengthwise so you have a skinny rectangle. Use your fingernail to crease the fold well. Open the paper so the unprinted side faces up. Fold all four corners in to the midline you made earlier, then fold the paper along the midline so the printed side faces out. It is now a trapezoid shape.

Fold the paper in half widthwise, then unfold it. Holding the trapezoid with the wider edge at the bottom, fold the two bottom corners in and up along the middle crease. Now your Patriotic Popper will take on a diamond shape. Turn the paper over and fold it in half toward you along the middle crease to make a triangle. Make sure all of your folds are creased well.

Hold the Patriotic Popper at the tip of the open end so that the long side of the triangle faces you. Raise your hand in the air and then bring your Popper down sharply. The paper will burst open and make a loud popping sound. This may take some practice. Try saying the following quick rhyme as families pop their Patriotic Poppers.

Thank you, God, for freedom true!
Thank you, God, for all you do!

As families practice, encourage them to talk about people they may have known who fought for their freedom.

Freedom Chalk

Simple Supplies: You'll need plaster of paris, 6-ounce paper drinking cups, measuring spoons, water, craft sticks for stirring, and food coloring in red and blue or other colors of your choosing.

Directions: Point out to families that the Fourth of July is a day to remember the Declaration of Independence, which states that all people are created equal and have the right to life, liberty, and the pursuit of happiness. American freedom from the king of England was declared over 200 years ago, but our spiritual freedom through God was declared before we were born! Decorate sidewalks and driveways in the days following the festival with this colored chalk as reminders of this twice-special day of freedom.

Hand each family member a paper cup and a craft stick. Direct festival-goers to measure 2 tablespoons of water into each cup. Then add 4 tablespoons of plaster of paris and quickly stir the ingredients until they're thick and smooth. Squirt 2 drops of food coloring into each cup, then swirl the color into the plaster mixture.

Set the cups of chalk aside to take home after the festival. Tell families to let their chalk dry for 24 hours, then peel away the paper cup. Use the chalk to decorate sidewalks, driveways, or even black construction paper! (This chalk washes off sidewalks with a water hose.)

FESTIVAL FOOD

Statue of Liberty Kabobs

Simple Supplies: You'll need pretzel sticks or bamboo skewers, whole fresh strawberries, large marshmallows, and whole fresh blueberries.

Directions: Encourage families to work together to make this festive treat, reminding them to continue thinking of ways they can celebrate freedom each day.

Give each person two pretzel sticks. Then stack a strawberry, a large marshmallow, and several blueberries on the pretzel sticks to create Statue of Liberty Kabobs. Explain to families that the red strawberry symbolizes God's offer of freedom through Jesus' blood. The white marshmallow symbolizes Christ's purity and forgiveness from sin. And the blueberries symbolize Jesus, the living water that sets us free.

Invite families to sit back and enjoy this sweet treat on a hot day. You may wish to serve lemonade along with this special summer snack. Be sure to have extra ingredients available—not many people can stop at just two Statue of Liberty Kabobs!

Patriotic Prayers

Simple Supplies: *You'll need Bibles and the Patriotic Poppers.*

Invite family groups to sit together. Have families open their Bibles to Joshua 1:1-9 and follow along as several volunteers read the passage aloud. Then ask everyone to point out ways God assured freedom for the Israelites and how God gave us his Son, Jesus, to set us free from sin and death. Encourage family groups to read John 3:16 aloud together. Then invite families to discuss these questions:

★ How is God an important part of our freedom? How is Jesus an important part?

★ How can we thank God for the freedom he offers us through Jesus?

Invite families to join in singing "I've Got a River of Life." Use the Patriotic Poppers to accompany your singing. Then close with a prayer thanking God for his gift of freedom. Encourage participants to name specific earthly and spiritual freedoms they're thankful for.

FAMILY FESTIVAL FOLLOW-UP

Thanks for Freedom

Extend your Freedom Festival celebration by having families write thank-you notes to people serving in the military overseas. After all, when was the last time you said thank-you to someone you don't even know who is far away from family and placing his life in danger to protect our freedoms? Send your thank-you notes to:

United Service Organizations, Inc.

Washington Navy Yard, Building 198

901 M Street SE

Washington, DC 20374

SUNDAY SUNDAE

Family
Faith Builder:

**Family
Faith Builder:**

Generosity

Generosity and ice-cream sundaes melt together for National Ice Cream Day.

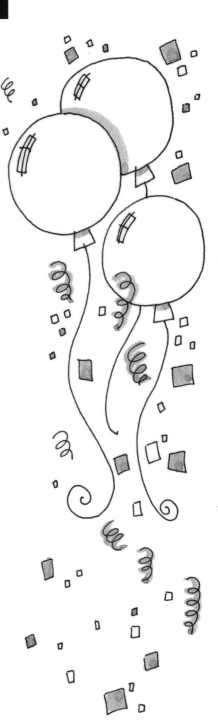

BIBLE BASIS: Ruth 2:11-23

A huge ice-cream sundae, dripping with chocolate sauce, covered with whipped cream, and topped with cherries is enough to make anyone's mouth water. But what does an enormous ice-cream sundae have to do with the story of Ruth? It all has to do with generosity. It's easy to give someone a spoonful of ice cream from an enormous sundae. When you have a lot, a little surely won't be missed. But how easy is it to be generous when you don't have much? Boaz and Ruth are wonderful examples of generosity who both gave out of their love for God and family. Celebrate National Ice Cream Day with generous ice-cream sundaes and the giving story of Ruth.

GETTING READY

Each activity in this family festival contains its own list of simple supplies. Simply choose and use the activities that fit your needs and time requirements, then gather the appropriate supplies. Use one or more of these decorating and invitation suggestions to enliven your special event:

★ Using colorful ribbon, attach small photocopied invitations to small ice-cream spoons. "Dish out" the spoons as families leave church several weeks before your festival.

★ Encourage families to bring an ice-cream topping to share with others during the Festival Food activity. You may even wish to create your own sundae bar out of the generous assortment of toppings.

★ Several weeks before the Sundae Sunday festival, begin a coloring contest by making photocopies of a scoop of ice cream in a cone. Encourage kids of all ages to color the picture and then name their own invented flavors of ice cream. The names should relate to a favorite Bible story—for example, Ruth's Raspberry Ripple, Noah's Rainbow Sherbet, or Tree of Life Tutti-Frutti. Award gift certificates donated from local ice cream stores as prizes.

★ Hold your festival outside at a picnic shelter or under the shade of several large trees. You'll also need to make sure you have picnic tables or indoor tables available for the Festival Crafts. If your festival falls on a hot July day, be sure to have plenty of water available!

★ Festival favors and prizes might include snack-sized boxes of cereal, cute spoons, ice-cream coupons, candy sprinkles, or colorful plastic bowls.

FESTIVAL GAMES

Gleaning the Wheat

Simple Supplies: You'll need popcorn, paper cups, tables, and drinking straws.

Directions: Remind participants that Boaz was very generous to let Ruth gather—or glean—the leftover grain from his fields. Point out that just as Ruth worked hard to glean the wheat, they'll work hard to glean their own grain in this lively game.

Have each person find a partner and stand on the opposite side of the table from his partner. Place a couple of handfuls of popcorn in the middle of the table in front of each pair. Give one partner a drinking straw and the other a paper cup. At the starting signal, encourage the partner with the straw to begin blowing the popcorn across the table. The partner holding the bowl will try to "glean" the grain by catching it in his bowl. Play until all the popcorn is in the bowls. If any popcorn falls, set it on the table for another try. The first pair to glean all of their grain wins the game.

Play again, but switch roles. Be sure to hand out new drinking straws!

Greedy Generosity

Simple Supplies: You'll need an assortment of wrapped candies and kitchen timers or stopwatches.

Directions: Tell families that this game may humorously point out just how generous or how greedy they can be.

Form circles of twelve or fewer people. Designate one person to be the timer. Place about twenty pieces of candy in front of the timer. Have the timer set the kitchen timer or stopwatch for any length of time up to 3 minutes. Explain that the object of this game is to pass the candies continuously around the circle. Players may elect to pass the candy to the next person or keep as much of a specific kind of candy as they would like. Begin the timer and begin passing pieces of candy around the circle. As soon as the first candy is passed, begin passing the next piece.

When the timer or stopwatch goes off, have players reveal how much, if any, candy they decided to keep. Briefly discuss why they chose to keep certain candies or pass the candies along. Then decide as a group how the candy should be divided. As you nibble pieces of candy, talk about feelings of generosity and greed, which you think God prefers, and why.

FESTIVAL CRAFTS

Ice-Cream Ornaments

Simple Supplies: You'll need thin ribbon, glue, scissors, ice-cream cones, polyester fiberfill, and small red pom-poms.

Directions: Point out that being generous at special times and holidays is often easier than remembering to be generous all year long. Explain that you'll be making Christmas ornaments in July to remind everyone that generosity isn't just for special days but for *every* day!

For each ornament, cut a 6-inch length of ribbon, then fold the ribbon in half and glue the ends inside the top edge of the cone. This will be the ornament hanger. Pull out a handful of polyester fiberfill and squeeze it into a ball about 3 inches in diameter. Squirt glue inside the rim of the ice-cream cone and poke the fiberfill into the top of the cone to make a "scoop" of ice cream. Finally, glue a small red pom-pom cherry on top of the ice cream.

As families work, encourage them to discuss ways they can show generosity to others. Then ask who they could generously present with their Ice-Cream Ornaments.

Grains-of-Wheat Potpourri

Simple Supplies: You'll need potpourri, 6-inch burlap squares, cracked wheat (available at health food stores), scissors, rubber bands, tablespoons, and ribbon.

Directions: Tell families that the Grains-of-Wheat Potpourri bag can be placed in the car as a constant reminder of God's generous love to Ruth and to us.

Give each person a square of burlap. Have participants place 1 or 2 tablespoons of potpourri and 1 tablespoon of cracked wheat in the centers of their squares. Demonstrate how to gather the corners of the burlap square up and secure them with a rubber band. Tie ribbons over the rubber bands, then hang the Grains-of-Wheat Potpourri sachets in a car or closet.

FESTIVAL FOOD

Sundae-in-a-Bag

Simple Supplies: You'll need milk, instant vanilla pudding mix, measuring spoons and cups, gallon and pint-sized resealable plastic freezer bags, ice, salt, and plastic spoons.

Directions: Explain that after families make this scrumptious treat, they may choose to generously give it to another person, just as Ruth did when she generously gave wheat to Naomi.

For each Sundae-in-a-Bag, measure 1 tablespoon of instant vanilla pudding mix and 1/2 cup of milk into a pint-sized resealable bag. Seal the bag and place it inside a gallon-sized resealable bag that has been half filled with ice and 6 tablespoons of salt. Seal the gallon bag securely. Carefully shake the bags for 5 minutes, then open the gallon bag and remove the smaller bag. Open the pint-sized bag and spoon on the toppings families brought to the festival to share. Eat your sundaes right out of the bag!

Festival Finesse

If some festival-goers want to make more than one Sundae-in-a-Bag, reuse the gallon bags with ice and salt.

FESTIVAL FINALE

Contagious Generosity

Simple Supplies: You'll need Bibles.

Invite family members to sit together. Have families open their Bibles to Ruth 2:11-23 and follow along as several volunteers read the passage aloud. Then ask people to point out ways generosity was shown to others in the passage. Have each family find a partner family and discuss these questions:

★ In what ways has God been generous to you?
★ How can generosity be contagious? How can greed be contagious?
★ When do your motives affect your generosity?
★ How can God help us act generously?

Encourage families to close by singing the following song as a prayer to the tune of "London Bridge Is Falling Down."

Give to others, kind and good,
Kind and good, kind and good.
Give to others, kind and good.
God will help us.

God wants us to share and care,
Share and care, share and care.
God wants us to share and care.
God will help us.

Givin' Go-fers

Before your Sundae Sunday festival, check with your church office or pastor to see if there are members of your congregation who could benefit from a little generosity. At the end of your festival, organize families to meet at another time and generously give of their time to go for groceries, wash windows, mow lawns, or pull weeds for those in need in your congregation or community. Make sure you also give generously of yourself by being a listening ear and caring heart for those you help.

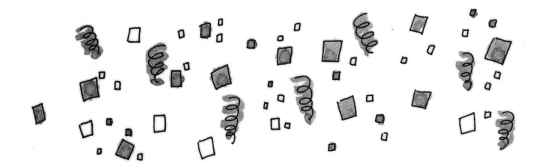

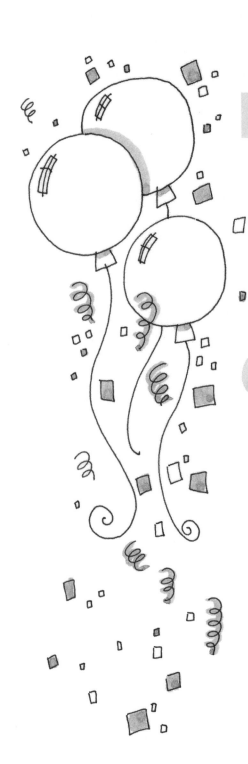

Family Faith Builder:

Happiness

SMILE AWHILE

Begin National Smile Week with a festival of fun to make you smile!

BIBLE BASIS: Psalm 98:1-9

What makes you smile? Is it a funny joke in a magazine or the toddler next door who says such funny things? The writer of Psalm 98 must have been smiling when he wrote this psalm. His happiness leaps off the page in this lilting psalm of praise to God! Psalm 98 also reminds us of a reason for our biggest smile yet—the knowledge of our salvation. So smile a while and celebrate National Smile Week in the middle of August with all your family and friends!

GETTING READY

Each activity in this family festival contains its own list of simple supplies. Simply choose and use the activities that fit your needs and time requirements, then gather the appropriate supplies. Use one or more of these decorating and invitation suggestions to enliven your special event:

★ Create unique invitations that will become happy memories of the Smile Awhile festival long after it's over. Glue a comic strip on one side of a piece of poster board or an index card. Photocopy the festival information and glue it to the other side of each invitation. Place a small piece of adhesive-backed magnetic strip on each side of the invitation. Invitations can be placed on the refrigerator to be enjoyed before and after the festival.

★ Ask festival helpers to dress in bright colors or even recruit a few jolly clowns.

★ Decorate your festival room to invite smiles when festival-goers enter the door. Polka dots on the walls are a nice touch to go along with the clown faces and brightly colored wigs or yarn hair festival workers can wear as guests arrive. Bright yellow balloons with smiley faces can be an extra happy touch too.

★ Cover the tables with funny papers or place colorful comic strips cut from newspapers on the tables.

★ Party prizes and favors might include smiley stickers, funny eyeglasses, balloons, and pretty "tickle-me" feathers!

FESTIVAL GAMES

Make-Me Smiles

Simple Supplies: You'll need Bibles.

Directions: Explain to families that they'll discover what made the author of Psalm 98 smile when he wrote this psalm and what can make them smile too.

Encourage families to sit in a large circle and designate three people to be the first smilers. Challenge the smilers to move around the circle from person to person trying to make people smile. Smilers cannot touch anyone—they must try to make people smile by gestures, words, smiles, or crazy giggles. If someone smiles, she also becomes a smiler. Play until everyone is a smiler.

When everyone is smiling or laughing, invite families to sit down and open their Bibles to Psalm 98. Ask a volunteer to read aloud verses 1 and 2 to see what made the author of this psalm smile. When you know the answer, point to your own smile and say, "God makes me smile too!" Briefly discuss why God makes us happy and how we can pass that joy to others, then give each other a hug for joy!

Happy Hunt

Simple Supplies: You'll need paper and pencils.

Directions: Remind families that they will get to know each other better as they play this game and that they are sure to have smiles on their faces when they're done.

Give each family a sheet of paper and a pencil. Then instruct families to secretly make a Happy Hunt list of five questions that will help them get to know another family better. Questions might include "What foods make you the happiest?" "Which family trip was your best?" "Which family holiday is your favorite?" and "What makes your family giggle?"

When the lists are complete, invite each family to join with another family and exchange questions and answers. When everyone is done, have people come back to the entire group and briefly tell why getting to know others makes them happy. Challenge families to take the time to meet others and to share their joy and love of God with each other during and after the festival.

Smile Paint

Simple Supplies: You'll need a Bible, cold cream, baby powder, food coloring, plastic spoons, cotton swabs, small paper cups, a pan of soapy water, and towels.

Directions: Ask families what they think a clown's job is. Then point out that clowns make people smile even when they don't feel much like smiling. Clowns paint their faces with happy expressions to pass joy to others. Explain that in this craft activity, they'll make special Smile Paint to paint joyous expressions too.

Give each family member a paper cup and a plastic spoon. Have participants measure 1 spoonful of cold cream and 1 spoonful of baby powder into their cups, then mix the ingredients thoroughly. At this point, participants may decide to keep their Smile Paints white or add 1 or 2 drops of food coloring to create colored paints.

Invite family members to decorate each other's faces or hands with Smile Paints, using cotton swabs as paintbrushes. If adults prefer not to be painted, encourage them to be the artists. Designs might include clouds and rainbows, butterflies, crosses, hearts, stars, and tiny balloons.

When faces are bubbling over with smiles, read aloud Psalm 98:1-6, then have families talk about spreading their love for God to others. Be sure to make a pan of soapy water and towels available for families to wash their hands after they're finished. Invite happy party participants to wear their Smile Paint throughout the entire festival.

Musical Smiles

Simple Supplies: You'll need scissors, markers, margarine tubs with plastic lids, paper plates, cardboard tubes, Tacky craft glue, tape, and a variety of the following decorating supplies: sequins, jingle bells, colored sticker dots, and uncooked rice.

Directions: Gather families and read aloud Psalm 98:4-6. Point out that the biblical author doesn't just tell us why he's happy but also how we can express our joy. Tell families they'll be inventing a variety of musical instruments to make everyone smile. Mention that you'll use these instruments of joy later in the festival.

Set out the craft materials and turn families—and their gleeful imaginations—loose! Suggest that families make shakers, rattlers, jinglers, or any other musical inventions they can think up. Tie the jingle bells along the edges of the plastic lids to make tambourines. Or turn plastic tubs upside down to make crazy drums to joyously thump on. Place uncooked rice in paper tubes and seal the ends with paper and tape to make rhythm shakers.

When families are finished with their musical contraptions, have them shake, rattle, and roll them a few times, then set them aside for later. Be sure people's initials are on their instruments.

FESTIVAL FOOD

Smile Sandwiches

Simple Supplies: You'll need bread, peanut butter, miniature marshmallows, raisins, squeeze-type jelly, plastic knives, napkins, paper plates and cups, and milk or lemonade.

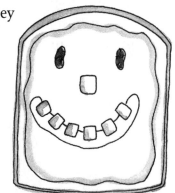

Directions: Tell families that they'll burst out into grins when they make these yummy Smile Sandwiches.

To make each Smile Sandwich, place a slice of bread on a paper plate. Spread a thin layer of peanut butter on one side of the bread. Add raisins as eyes and a miniature marshmallow as a nose. Finally, make a happy jelly smile on the sandwich. If family members are feeling exceptionally happy, suggest that they make an extra-wide jelly smile and add miniature-marshmallow teeth for a toothy grin! Serve this yummy snack with frosty milk or chilled lemonade.

FESTIVAL FINALE

Psalm Smiles

Simple Supplies: You'll need Bibles and the musical instruments you made earlier.

Invite family groups to sit together. Have families open their Bibles to Psalm 98 and read the psalm in unison. Ask everyone to point out ways the biblical author expressed his happiness in this psalm. Then have family groups discuss one or more of the following questions:

★ In what ways does loving God make us happy?

★ How does God's plan for salvation through Jesus bring us joy?

★ What can you do to help others smile this week?

Read Psalm 98:4-6 again, then sing "This Is the Day" several times as participants play their musical instruments. If you wish, sing the song as a round for a great finale. Then close with a prayer thanking God for his wonderful world and his promise of salvation, which most definitely makes us smile!

Operation Smile

Operation Smile is an international organization that helps poor children around the world who have burns or scars on their faces that keep them from smiling. Doctors and nurses volunteer to perform operations to correct the problems. Many of these children stay in hospitals for a long time after their surgeries. Families can become involved by making Smile Bags, each filled with a comb, a tube of toothpaste, a toothbrush, a small container of shampoo, and a small toy. These bags can be given to the children participating in Operation Smile by mailing them to:

Operation Smile
220 Boush Street
Norfolk, VA 23510

IN A PICKLE

Celebrate the lowly pickle—while learning about the pickle Job was in!

BIBLE BASIS: Job 1:13-17

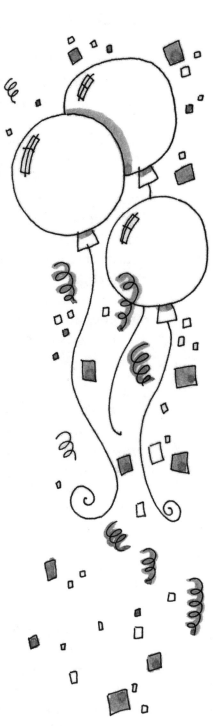

The pickle is an odd kind of food. It begins as a fresh, crisp, juicy cucumber just as God intended it to be. Then people turn right around and cook it in sour vinegar, or brine, where the cucumber gets soggy, shrivels up, and becomes a pickle. The cucumber has to endure a lot to become a pickle. In a similar way, if you are "in a pickle," you're most likely caught in the middle of the "brine" of life. Job was in such a pickle, but he persevered through it all and continued to praise God. Celebrate National Pickle Day in the middle of August and help families learn that perseverance prevails!

GETTING READY

Each activity in this family festival contains its own list of simple supplies. Simply choose and use the activities that fit your needs and time requirements, then gather the appropriate supplies. Use one or more of these decorating and invitation suggestions to enliven your special event:

★ Photocopy invitations on green construction paper, then cut them out in the shape of pickles.

★ Hang green streamers and green construction-paper pickles from the ceiling of your festival room. Cover the tables with green paper and place several cucumbers on the tables as centerpieces.

★ Ask families to bring jars of uniquely flavored or homemade pickles that are family favorites. Arrange the jars around the room for added decoration and to be eaten later in the festival. Be sure you have a variety of sweet and sour pickles!

★ As families arrive, encourage them to create their own Pickle-Twisters, tongue-twisters with a pucker. "Peter Piper picked a peck of pickled peppers" may not stand a chance against Pickle-Twisters such as, "Pretty pickles persevere past plucky people" or "Pink pickles pluck piccolos preposterously."

★ Perky party favors might include jars of pickles, cucumbers, small packets of salad dressing, or plastic pickle forks.

FESTIVAL GAMES

Shoe-Pile Pickle

Simple Supplies: You'll need cucumbers with the numbers 1, 2, and 3 written on them with markers and the shoes that people are wearing.

Directions: Explain what perseverance is and how it helps us. Then tell families that they'll need perseverance to find their shoes and put them back on in this wild game.

Instruct people to remove their shoes and pile them together in the middle of the playing area. Ask a volunteer to scramble up the shoe pile. Place the numbered cucumbers about 15 feet away from the shoes, then have participants stand near the cucumbers. Explain that at the starting signal, families race to find and put on their shoes. Families must remain at the shoe pile until all of their family members' shoes are on and tied or buckled, so small children may need their family's help! When everyone in a family has his shoes on, have the entire family race to the numbered cucumbers and pick them up in order of first, second, and third places.

If there's time for a second round, try this twist! Have pairs race to find their partner's shoes and put them on their feet.

Givers and Takers

Simple Supplies: You'll need a paper pickle for each player and several pennies. You'll also need a green pencil for each participant to keep. Pencils need not have green lead.

Directions: Tell families that even after Job had lost almost everything, he declared, "The Lord gave and the Lord has taken away; may the name of the Lord be praised" (Job 1:21). Job persevered even when the going got rough. Explain that this game will remind family members to be thankful no matter what their circumstances may be.

Have people form a circle, then give each person either a penny or a paper pickle. Explain that in this game of give and take, players may ask for what another player has and the player being asked must exchange items willingly. Both players must say, "Thank you for the (penny or pickle)." Then the next player in the circle may ask for an item. Tell players that at the end of the game, players with pennies receive prizes.

Continue around the circle until everyone has had at least two chances to ask for an item. Call time, then see which item everyone has. Explain that before prizes are given out, festival-goers are to discuss how it felt to get a paper pickle when they had a valuable penny. Remind everyone that Job had things of great value in his life before they were taken away but that he persevered and praised God even when he had nothing. And in the end, God rewarded him. Reward all players—those with pennies and with pickles—with green pencils as prizes.

FESTIVAL CRAFTS

Bumpy Pickles

Simple Supplies: You'll need tongue depressors, Tacky craft glue, green markers, adhesive-backed magnetic strips, and blow-dryers.

Directions: Remind families that the cucumber perseveres through many steps to become a bumpy pickle. They'll need a little perseverance to create these pickles!

Hand a tongue depressor to each person. Show participants how to squeeze glue dots (or pickle bumps) down the length of the tongue depressors. Then quickly blow-dry the glue to create hard, raised bumps on the sticks. Have adults help small children with the drying.

When the bumps are dry, use green markers to color the bumpy sides of the sticks green. Attach pieces of adhesive-backed magnetic strip to the backs of the Bumpy Pickles. Encourage families to talk about people who have persevered much and relied on God. Tell families to place their bumpy pickle magnets where they'll see them often and be reminded to praise God for all they have.

Puzzler Pins

Simple Supplies: You'll need puzzle pieces, paper plates, small craft pins (available at craft stores), Tacky craft glue, and various sequins, buttons, glitter, or seed beads.

Directions: Point out that even though it may have been puzzling for Job to experience all he was going through, he persevered through it and trusted God. Remind everyone that we don't always understand what God is doing in our lives but that we need to persevere and trust him. These pins will remind families not to puzzle over their troubles but to persevere and trust God through them.

Give each person a paper plate. Instruct people to work over their plates so small items do not roll on the table or floor. Invite participants to select several puzzle pieces and use the glue to join them together in an overlapping manner. Blow on the puzzle

Festival Finesse

Families may want to use fine-tipped permanent markers to write Job 1:21b ("May the name of the Lord be praised") on the backs of their Bumpy Pickles or Puzzler Pins when they're dry.

pieces to dry them a bit. Adorn the puzzle pieces with sequins, beads, glitter, or small buttons. While families work, have them discuss ways they must persevere each day.

Finally, attach a craft pin to the back of each Puzzler Pin, then set the pins aside to dry before wearing.

FESTIVAL FOOD

Pickle Dip

Simple Supplies: You'll need mayonnaise or salad dressing, grated Parmesan cheese, season salt, measuring spoons, plastic spoons, and 6-ounce paper cups. You'll also need sliced cucumbers, carrots, celery chunks, and the jars of pickles that families brought to the festival.

Directions: Pucker up for a tasty treat! Give each person a paper cup and a spoon. To prepare the Pickle Dip, spoon 1 tablespoon of mayonnaise (or salad dressing) into each cup. Add 1 teaspoon of Parmesan cheese and 1/4 teaspoon of season salt to the mayonnaise. Mix the ingredients well. Invite festival-goers to dip cucumbers and assorted raw vegetables into their Pickle Dip for a tasty treat. They may even want to experiment by dipping a pickle or two into the dip. If not, pickles can be eaten by themselves!

FESTIVAL FINALE

Pucker-Up Perseverance

Simple Supplies: You'll need Bibles, napkins, and sweet and sour pickles.

Hand family members napkins and invite everyone to select a sour and a sweet pickle. Then have families open their Bibles to Job and follow along as a volunteer reads Job 1:13-17. Each time Job loses something in his life, have everyone take a bite of the sour pickle. Then have everyone say, "Thank you, God. May the name of the Lord be praised!" and take a bite of the sweet pickle. Repeat the process throughout the passage, then remind families that even when things were bad for Job, he continued to persevere and praise God.

Have family groups discuss one or more of these questions:

★ When are times you have been called upon to persevere?

★ Who helps you persevere when you want to give up?

★ How can perseverance help your faith in God grow?

Encourage families to make a list at home of areas in their lives in which they need to persevere just as Job did. Then close with a prayer asking God's strength when we need perseverance and thanking him for loving us.

FAMILY FESTIVAL FOLLOW-UP

Exodus World Service

Here's a chance for festival families to help groups of people who must persevere when moving to the United States. Become involved in the "Welcome to America" project offered through Exodus World Service to help refugee families adjust during their first month in America. This project collects food staples and household items to be used directly by new refugee families. For more information on how your family can help, call the Exodus World Service at 1-708-307-1400.

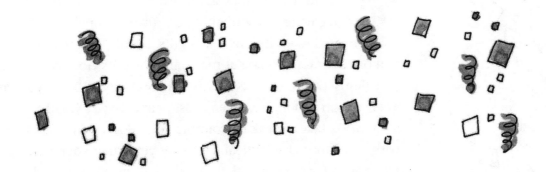

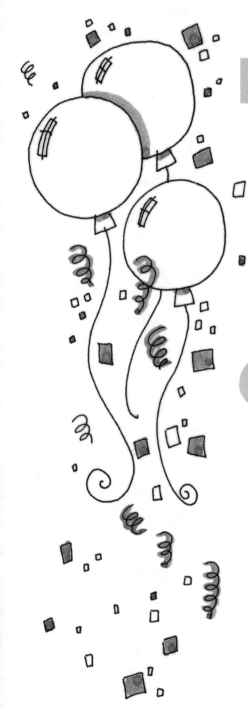

Family Faith Builder:

Stewardship

LABOR DAY

Invest your time, talents, and treasures in God's service.

BIBLE BASIS: Matthew 25:14-29

The dictionary defines stewardship as "the careful and responsible management of something entrusted to one's care." God has entrusted to each of us many gifts, talents, and treasures. How are you or your family doing at managing the gifts God has entrusted to you? Jesus' parable of the Talents is a good way to begin your analysis! This year on Labor Day, when most people have a holiday from their daily work, take a break to examine your God-given gifts by celebrating with this Labor Day Festival. Or better yet, when your congregation is planning a fund drive, kick it off with this exciting festival!

GETTING READY

Each activity in this family festival contains its own list of simple supplies. Simply choose and use the activities that fit your needs and time requirements, then gather the appropriate supplies. Use one or more of these decorating and invitation suggestions to enliven your special event:

★ Photocopy Labor Day festival invitations in the shape of pennies on brown construction paper.

★ Encourage families to bring their extra pennies to the Labor Day festival. Set up a "Penny Wash" station for families to work on as they arrive at the festival. Dip the pennies in vinegar, then sprinkle them with salt. Gently rub the pennies between two paper towels and... oh, they'll look so shiny and new! Use the pennies for the Festival Games.

★ Decorate your festival area by hanging brown or copper-colored penny circles from the ceiling. You may even want to make a whole bank full of green dollar bills to attach to walls and spread on the floor throughout the room. Toss make-believe money on party tables for a whimsical touch.

★ When advertising your festival, hand out green construction-paper bills or children's play money. Encourage families to bring this money to be used during the Festival Finale.

★ Festival favors and prizes might include shiny pennies, chocolate coins, and plastic piggy banks.

FESTIVAL GAMES

Pennies From Heaven

Simple Supplies: You'll need small paper cups and ten pennies for each family.

Directions: Remind families that God has given us all we have. Point out that it's important to use our time, talents, and money to serve God and that God wants us to be good stewards of all that he has given us. This game will remind everyone that their pennies come, literally, from heaven!

Hand each player a paper cup. Have each family form a group and hand each family ten pennies. Instruct each family to choose one member to be the flipper and designate the rest as catchers. At your signal, have the flippers turn their backs to the catchers and then flip one penny at a time into the air. The family catchers must try to catch the penny in their cups. If a penny falls to the ground, it must be retrieved and flipped again before another penny is launched. The first family to catch all their "pennies from heaven" wins.

Play several times, choosing new flippers for each round. When the game is over, encourage families to talk about ways they can use pennies, nickels, and dimes to serve God.

Talent Search

Simple Supplies: You'll need pencils and copies of the Talent Search grid. See illustration for the grid outline.

Directions: Remind families that God has given each of them unique talents that can be used to serve him. Ask participants to name what kinds of talents God gives people. Then play this fun get-to-know-you game to search for the hidden talents each person has.

Distribute a Talent Search grid and pencil to each family member. Younger children who cannot write may "buddy-up" with Mom, Dad, or an older sibling. Encourage families to mingle with other festival-goers to search out the talents that six people might have to fill in the spaces on their grids. Talents could

What's Your Talent?	
Name	Talent
1	
2	
3	
4	
5	
6	

include playing softball, writing, reading, or even finding the best sales when shopping. No talent is insignificant or unusable for God! Encourage participants to sign their names on each grid square as they discuss their talents with others. The first person with a filled grid is the winner. However, encourage everyone to continue until all the grids are full.

Gather into one group and invite participants to talk about some of the talents they discovered in their Talent Search. Visit about ways they can use these talents to serve God. Is there an area in their church or a service group that could use their talents?

FESTIVAL CRAFTS

Sock-It-Away Banks

Simple Supplies: You'll need self-hardening clay (available from craft stores), aluminum foil, and dried peas or gumdrop halves. Use scissors to snip gumdrops in half prior to the festival.

Directions: Explain to families that they can combine their talents in creating these cool Sock-It-Away Banks to be used to collect the family's spare change.

To make each bank, begin with a piece of self-hardening clay the size of a golf ball. Roll the clay into a smooth ball, then flatten it between your palms. Be sure the clay is no thinner than 1/2 inch. Poke your thumb through the center of the clay pancake to make a mouth. If you would like, slightly pinch the "lips" for a funny effect. Be sure the mouth openings are large enough for coins to slide through. Poke dried peas or gumdrop halves into the clay to make eyes or noses. Then place your clay face on a piece of aluminum foil to take home.

The clay should harden in several hours. When it's hard, families are to glue the bottom edge of each face to an old sock—with no holes, please! Then families can have fun "feeding" their Sock-It-Away Banks any spare change they might have. Challenge families to cooperatively collect their spare change for the next three months, then donate their treasures to a local service organization. What an easy way to serve God and help others!

Talented Twisters

Simple Supplies: You'll need paper plates, scissors, rulers, paper punches, lightweight string or yarn, and crayons or markers.

Directions: Point out to families that we need to practice some of the talents God gives us if we want them to be productive. Explain that using our time and talents in a good way is often very hard work and that making these fun twisty toys will take a bit of time and talent to make them work.

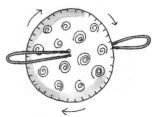

Hand a paper plate to each person. Then measure and cut out a 5-inch circle from each plate.

Have each person use markers or crayons to decorate both sides of her circle. Then use a paper punch to make two holes close together and near the center of each circle. Cut a 30-inch piece of string for each circle and thread it through the two holes. Tie the ends of the string to make a big loop. Demonstrate how to hold the two ends of the string loop with your index fingers, with the circle in the middle like a wheel. Twirl or rotate your wrists quickly to twist the string, then pull the string taut to untwist it—and watch the Talented Twister spin! It might take a little practice to be a talented twister or twistette!

 **FESTIVAL FOOD**

Copper Pennies

Simple Supplies: You'll need round butter-flavored snack crackers, creamy peanut butter, processed cheese spread in a can, plastic knives, napkins, paper plates and cups, and chilled fruit juice.

Directions: Tell families that good stewards use their time wisely in their service to God. Point out that cooperation such as you'd find in an assembly line is a good use of time and talent. So set up an assembly line to create edible Copper Pennies in a snap!

Have families determine which of the following jobs each of the members will have. Each family will need a tosser, a taker, a spreader, and a topper. The tosser will place two crackers for each family member on a separate paper plate or napkin. The taker will put a small amount of cheese spread on one cracker and a small amount of peanut butter on the other. The spreader will spread the toppings on each cracker before the topper places another cracker on top of each. The Copper Pennies are now ready to eat. Serve the copper pennies with chilled fruit juice and visit about ways to serve God even when you don't seem to have much time.

  **FESTIVAL FINALE**

Give Your Gifts

Simple Supplies: You'll need Bibles, pencils or pens, and the green construction-paper money or play money that was distributed before the festival. Have extra play money available if families have forgotten to bring back their bucks.

Invite each family group to find a quiet place to sit. Have families follow along in their Bibles as several volunteers read Matthew 25:14-29 aloud. Ask participants to point out ways the servants used the money that was given to them and which servant used his money in the best way. Then challenge family groups to discuss these questions:

★ How do you use your talents to serve God?

★ Why is it important to be good stewards of your time and talents?

★ How can your family use their cooperative gifts, time, and talents to serve God and others?

Be sure everyone has a paper dollar and a pen or pencil. Encourage each family member to write on the back of the paper money one gift of time or one talent she could give someone in the family. Suggested gifts and talents could include the gift of ten minutes of peace and quiet, the gift of reading a book to you, or the talent of helping in the garden. Exchange the paper bills within the family, promising to share those gifts in the coming week. Then close with a prayer thanking God for his gifts of time, talent, and treasures and for his guidance in the stewardship of all of them.

FAMILY FESTIVAL FOLLOW-UP

Habitat for Humanity

Anyone can build a house, right? Well, it's not that easy. But anyone regardless of age or talent can become involved in this important outreach organization that builds homes for the needy. Habitat for Humanity has built over 60,000 homes worldwide for families who could in no other way own a home. As a family, you can donate your time, talents, and treasures, and you don't have to do any heavy construction work! To participate in any way, call 1-888-BUILD-100 for more information.

OLD TIME FUN!

Celebrate Grandparent's Day with love and laughter.

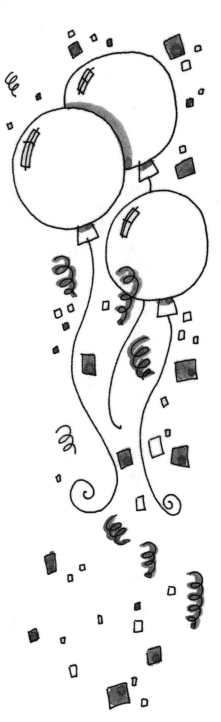

BIBLE BASIS: Exodus 20:12; Romans 12:10

"Gray hair is a crown of honor." "Honor your father and mother." "Respect your elders." These sayings all point to the importance of nurturing, honoring, and respecting those who are older than you. Begin a worthwhile family tradition by celebrating Grandparent's Day during the second week of September to honor and respect the seniors in your midst. Bring along your grandma or gramps or adopt a grandparent for the evening, and come to this fun family festival to share a time of honoring, reminiscing with, and appreciating seniors.

GETTING READY

Each activity in this family festival contains its own list of simple supplies. Simply choose and use the activities that fit your needs and time requirements, then gather the appropriate supplies. Use one or more of these decorating and invitation suggestions to enliven your special event:

★ Find an old-fashioned photo to use as an invitation for this evening of fun. Write the details to the Good Ol' Days festival on the back and then photocopy the invitations.

★ As you advertise your Good Ol' Days festival at church, wear a pair of overalls or an old-fashioned dress. Carry a basket with invitations and silk flowers to put families in the mood to celebrate with old-fashioned fun.

★ Encourage families (and especially grandparents!) to bring photo albums, old toys, or antique "whatchamacallits" to the festival.

★ Prior to the festival, arrange to have a grandmother or grandfather read or tell childhood stories to children as they arrive. A rocking chair with an afghan draped over it lends a nice atmosphere.

★ Festival favors and prizes could include boxes of old-fashioned Cracker Jack snacks, chenille wires to make "granny glasses," and silk flowers.

FESTIVAL GAMES

Tell Me a Story

Simple Supplies: You'll need beginning story-line questions written on slips of paper before your festival begins.

Directions: Before the festival, write story-line questions on slips of paper. Make sure you have one story-line question for each person. You can make several copies of the same story lines. Examples of beginning story-line questions could include "What's one thing you've never done that you would really like to do?" "What's your favorite Bible story?" "If you could live in any other time in history, when would you choose?" "If you had to spend the rest of your life on a deserted island, who and what five things would you take?"

Point out to families that they can show honor to others, including their own grand-parents, when they share or listen to stories about their lives. Form intergenerational groups of two or three. Have people each take a story-line question and tell their answers. Encourage partners to ask more questions if they'd like. If partners finish quickly, encourage them to select another story line or make up one of their own. You'll learn so much about and from each other!

R-E-S-P-E-C-T

Simple Supplies: You'll need paper lunch sacks, 5-foot lengths of yarn, and Cheerios or Froot Loops cereal.

Directions: Explain to families that they can respect each other by playing this game in the spirit of fun.

Form family groups and hand each a 5-foot piece of yarn and a bag of cereal loops. Instruct each family to tie a cereal loop to one end of their yarn. Then have family members line up next to each other. Explain that the object of this game is to be the first group to completely string its yarn with cereal loops by spelling out the word respect. Tell everyone that, at the starting signal, the first person in line strings a cereal loop on the yarn, saying R as he or she

passes the yarn to the next person in line. This player strings a loop and says E. Continue stringing cereal and spelling the word respect. After families spell respect once, they are to continue spelling it over and over until the yarn piece is completely filled. The first team to fill the yarn with cereal wins.

After the game, have families briefly discuss the differences and similarities between honor and respect and list ways they can honor their grandparents or other senior citizens.

FESTIVAL CRAFTS

Through God's Eyes

Simple Supplies: *You'll need round toothpicks, assorted colors of embroidery floss cut into 2-foot lengths, and Tacky craft glue.*

Directions: Several days before the Good Ol' Days festival, glue the toothpicks together in cross shapes, using two for each cross. Tacky craft glue or hot glue will keep the toothpicks securely fastened.

Point out that God's eyes are always upon us and that God knows how we treat others. God knows when we treat others kindly and with respect as well as when we treat them unkindly or impatiently. Remind families that God wants us to honor and respect others, especially parents and grandparents. Wind and wrap these colorful ornaments to remind people that God smiles when we respect and care for others.

Hand each person a toothpick cross. Younger children may need help from an adult to complete this craft. Invite each family member to choose a favorite color of embroidery floss. Tie one end of the floss around one arm of the cross, near the center. Then wrap the floss in a clockwise direction, wrapping under and around one arm of the toothpick and over and around the next arm of the toothpick. Remind families to keep the floss taut. Your Through God's Eyes ornament is complete when the toothpick cross is entirely wrapped with floss. Finish off your decoration by tying the floss off in a loop to be used as a hanger.

Honor Autograph Books

Simple Supplies: *You'll need colored copier paper, colored poster board, crayons, markers, stickers, a stapler, and pens.*

Directions: Before your festival begins, cut the colored copier paper and colored poster board into 4-by-6-inch pieces. You'll need eight pieces of the paper and two pieces of poster board for each person.

Tell participants that others will think it's an honor to write their names inside these special Honor Autograph Books.

95

Invite families to compile their copier papers into miniature books with poster-board covers. Staple the book along the left edge. Decorate the book covers with markers, crayons, and stickers.

When the Honor Autograph Books are ready for honorable signatures, have festival-goers mill around and ask as many people as they can to sign their books. Encourage people to write brief messages, happy thoughts, or Scripture verses or references beside their names. As participants open their Honor Autograph Books in the coming weeks, they'll be able to look up in their Bibles and read the favorite verses of Grandma or neighbor Bill as part of their daily devotions.

FESTIVAL FOOD

Cream of the Crop!

Simple Supplies: You'll need cans of sliced peaches (or sliced fresh peaches), several quarts of cream, small wafer cookies, disposable bowls, napkins, and plastic spoons.

Directions: Explain that a favorite old-fashioned treat and dessert is peaches and cream. But many children have never tasted this special treat their grandparents loved!

Spoon several peach slices into a disposable bowl and pour a bit of whole cream over the top. Stick two wafer cookies in the bowl and gobble your treats using plastic spoons. As you enjoy this old-fashioned treat, invite grandparents and older participants to tell some of their favorite childhood memories. Encourage everyone to ask questions. End snack time by asking a volunteer to say a special prayer asking God's blessings upon grandparents and senior citizens.

FESTIVAL FINALE

Honor One Another

Simple Supplies: You'll need Bibles and the photo albums brought to the festival.

Invite family groups to find a quiet place to sit together. Explain that as several verses from the Bible are read, families are to listen to find out who we should respect and honor. Have volunteers read aloud the following Scripture verses: Exodus 20:12; Romans 12:10; and 1 Peter 2:17. Then ask who these verses tell us to honor and respect. Remind families that respecting others includes the members in our families, as well as neighbors, teachers, friends, and people we may not even know. Challenge family groups to discuss one or more of these questions:

★ In what ways can we respect and honor God?
★ Why is it important to respect and honor older people?
★ How can you develop more respect within your family?

Encourage all generations of each family to honor one another by looking at the photograph albums they may have brought with them. Don't rush this part of the festival. A new appreciation and respect for each member of the family will develop as memories are shared. Close with a prayer thanking God for grandparents, families, and their relationships with each other and with God.

FAMILY FESTIVAL FOLLOW-UP

Write Partner

The relationship and friendship between grandchildren and their grandparents can be a wonderful thing. Do you feel as though you or your family has missed out on getting to know a grandfather figure in your life? If so, here's your chance to get to know a grandma or grandpa in the United States. Write Partner will match you up with a senior citizen who will write letters to you if you send letters in return. All generations can benefit from this wonderful project! Contact:

Write Partner
Family Literacy Center
2805 E. 10th St., #150
Bloomington, IN 47408

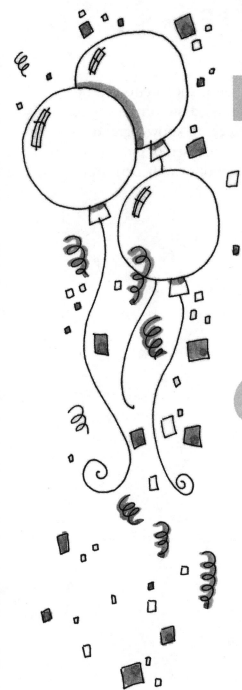

**Family
Faith Builder:**

Kindness

NATIONAL GROUCH DAY

Throw away the gloomies and discover kindness.

BIBLE BASIS: Matthew 19:13-15

Your day is going from bad to worse. You're getting grumpier and grumpier. Then someone shows a bit of kindness. Isn't it amazing how one small act of kindness can change the entire day? The disciples didn't want children bothering Jesus and tried to shoo them away. But Jesus' kindness prevailed, and the children were welcomed with open arms. Jesus' one small act of kindness and his concern for children became an important part of his ministry. So "celebrate" National Grouch Day in mid-October by showing family kindness.

GETTING READY

Each activity in this family festival contains its own list of simple supplies. Simply choose and use the activities that fit your needs and time requirements, then gather the appropriate supplies. Use one or more of these decorating and invitation suggestions to enliven your special event:

★ Have you seen those happy-face pins, buttons, and shirts? Start your own advertising trend for National Grouch Day by making cardboard buttons with humorous grouchy faces on them. Glue photocopied invitations to the backs of the buttons, then attach a large pin at the top as a visible reminder of your clever Grouch Day festival.

★ Take black-and-white photos of church members with humorous grouchy faces in the weeks before the festival. Decorate your festival room with the photos. As families arrive, encourage them to vote for the grumpiest face or write humorous conversation balloons to accompany each picture. You may want to playfully award the winning entries with packages of sourball candies.

★ Decorate the room with plenty of happy, grumpy, sleepy, and laughing balloons. Simply draw a variety of faces and expressions on colorful balloons and suspend them from ceilings, doorways, tables, and chairs.

★ Party prizes and favors might include smiley pins and erasers, coupons for Good Humor ice-cream bars, and cheery balloons.

FESTIVAL GAMES

Give a Grouch a Smile!

Simple Supplies: You'll need twenty paper plates, tape, markers, a cassette of lively music, and a cassette player.

Directions: Draw grumpy faces on fifteen of the paper plates and make the other five happy and smiling. If your group is larger than twenty-one, either add more plates or make two sets of grumpy and smiley plates. Tape the plates to the floor in a circle, alternating a smiley plate with several grumpy plates. Tape the plates about 1 foot apart.

Remind families that we have many emotions, then ask them to name emotions, such as happiness, sadness, confusion, and grumpiness. Point out that there are days we may feel grumpy but that we don't want to spread that grumpiness to others. In this game, players will have the opportunity to choose grumpiness or kindness.

Tell participants that this game is played much like musical chairs. Invite each person to stand on a paper plate. When the music begins, have players step from plate to plate around the circle. When the music stops, everyone needs to freeze on the plate they're on. Players on smiley faces are safe. But players on a grumpy face are out unless someone on a smiley plate is willing to exchange places. Players who are out go to the center of the circle to cheer others on. Begin the music again and continue playing until there is only one player left or all remaining players are on smiley plates.

After several rounds, discuss why some players gave up their safe places to those who landed on grumpy faces. Ask players how it felt to give up their places or to be offered a happy face. Remind everyone that happiness is a choice we make every day. Explain that loving God helps us make kind choices and spread happiness to those who may be having a grumpy day!

Tickle Me Happy

Simple Supplies: You'll need colorful craft feathers.

Directions: Point out that the great thing about smiles and laughter is the way they spread! It's tough to keep frowning when you feel like clowning!

Have people line up at one end of the playing area. Hand each person a craft feather.

Choose someone to be the tickler and have that person stand opposite everyone else, about 20 feet away. Explain that when the tickler tosses the feather in the air, everyone begins walking forward and smiling or laughing. Why, they can even tickle their neighbors with their feathers to get extra smiles! But when the tickler's feather lands on the floor, everyone freezes in place and has to make a grumpy face—if they can! Anyone caught moving, laughing, giggling, or smiling must go back and begin again. The first person to catch the tickler's feather becomes the next tickler.

Play the game several times, choosing new ticklers often. Then sit in a large group and briefly discuss why it was hard to stop smiling and laughing. Remind families that smiles and laughter are so catching that its hard to frown! End with a group tickle, then let families keep their pretty feathers to use as happy reminders that one smile is worth more than a million frowns.

FESTIVAL CRAFTS

Salty-Face Smiles

Simple Supplies: *You'll need empty spice shaker containers, sturdy paper plates, pencils, newspaper, several bottles of glue, and different colors of salt. (You can make your own by shaking together 2 teaspoons of powdered tempera paint with 1/4 cup salt.) Place the colored salt in the shaker containers.*

Directions: Remind families that Jesus showed kindness to the little children, even when others were grumpy. These smiley-face projects will remind families of how the children's faces must have looked when Jesus was kind and loving to them.

Cover a table with newspapers and set out the craft materials. Hand each person a paper plate and a pencil. Draw faces with happy expressions and big smiles on the paper plates, then cover the pencil marks with lines of glue squeezed from the glue bottles. When all of the facial features are traced with glue, shake colored salt over the glue lines. Shake the excess salt from each face by pouring it onto a spare paper plate. Some will love using the leftover multicolored salt for their faces!

As families are finishing their Salty Faces, have them talk about ways others know when they are grouchy or when they are happy. What other things clue people in to our moods? Remind everyone that Jesus showed kindness to the children and to the adults and that we can show kindness to others too.

Grouch-Pouch

Simple Supplies: *You'll need colorful balloons, small funnels, flour or baking powder, measuring cups, and black permanent markers.*

Directions: Tell families that they can squeeze a Grouch-Pouch when they're feeling grumpy inside. A Grouch-Pouch can help release the stress inside so kindness can rush out!

Have family members work together to create this craft—some steps require several pairs of helping hands. Give each family member a balloon. Have people inflate the balloons, then release the air. (The balloons need to be stretched out before proceeding to the next step.) Place a funnel in the opening of each balloon. Have one family member hold the balloon neck tightly to the funnel as another person carefully scoops 1/2 cup of flour or baking powder into the balloon. Carefully pull the neck of the balloon away from the funnel and tie it in a knot.

Use markers to draw comical grouchy faces on one or both sides of the balloons. Then squeeze and mash and crumple these goofy grumpies—you may even get *them* to smile!

FESTIVAL FOOD

Sweet-and-Sour Sandwiches

Simple Supplies: You'll need vanilla wafer cookies, nondairy whipped topping, sour gummy disks or worms, plastic spoons, and napkins.

Directions: Point out that these sandwiches remind us of sweet kindness and sour, pucker-up grouchiness all at one time. Hopefully the sweet kindness of this treat will prevail!

Hand two vanilla cookies to each person. Have people place a small dollop of whipped topping on each of the cookies, then a sour gummy disk or a curled gummy worm on the whipped topping. Place the two cookies together to make a Sweet-and-Sour Sandwich. Now nibble and enjoy! Many festival-goers will want to make more than one sandwich treat.

As you nibble away, encourage families to discuss what things tend to make them grumpy and what things make them happy. Have families tell reasons that Jesus makes them smile and how they can pass on that joy to others who might not know Jesus.

FESTIVAL FINALE

Acts of Kindness

Simple Supplies: You'll need Bibles, pencils, and paper.

Invite family groups to sit together, open their Bibles to Matthew 19:13-15, and follow along as a volunteer reads the passage aloud. Ask everyone to point out ways Jesus showed kindness to the children and why Jesus might have acted in this way. Then have family groups think about and discuss these questions:

★ What can you do to change your attitude during grouchy times?

★ What does it mean when we say that "happiness is a choice we make every day"? Is grumpiness a choice too? Explain.

★ What are ways we can spread kindness to others?

Give each family a piece of paper and a pencil. Encourage families to make a list of some random acts of kindness they could do this week for someone in the neighborhood, church, or family. Point out that random acts of kindness are kind things we can do for someone else, such as delivering cookies to an ill neighbor, giving away a Grouch-Pouch your family made, recycling or picking up litter, or simply giving someone a friendly call on the telephone. Challenge families to be creative when making their lists.

Close with a prayer asking God for a change of heart when festival-goers feel grouchy and for help to show kindness to others all the time. End with a kind family hug.

FAMILY FESTIVAL FOLLOW-UP

Kindness Counts

Okay, here's a chance for your family to put into action all of those acts of kindness that were compiled during the Festival Finale! Don't just bring the list home and lose it— use it! Put your list in a prominent place and refer to it often during the week. Being kind to others can become a wonderful family habit. And those grouchy times won't have many chances to pop up when you're being kind to others!

ALL SAINTS' EVE

Rejoice in life at this alternative Halloween celebration.

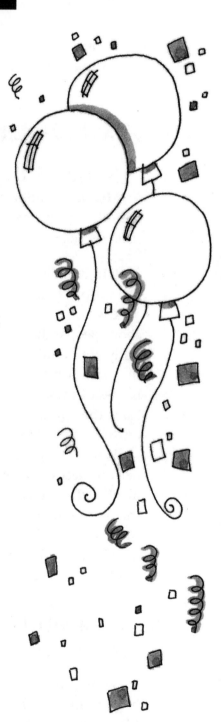

BIBLE BASIS: Acts 12:3-18; Philippians 1:3-11

It's Halloween, and doorbells ring as children travel from house to house costumed and ready for fun. What began as a pagan holiday has turned into a secular celebration, but many parents would like to offer an alternative to this traditional night of trick-or-treating. This All Saints' Eve celebration offers a peaceful, Christ-centered alternative to Halloween and the chance to celebrate a night long ago when early Christians roamed dark streets, peacefully guarded by God's angels. Celebrate all God's saints on the night before All Saints' Day, November 1.

GETTING READY

Each activity in this family festival contains its own list of simple supplies. Simply choose and use the activities that fit your needs and time requirements, then gather the appropriate supplies. Use one or more of these decorating and invitation suggestions to enliven your special event:

★ Encourage festival-goers to wear costumes depicting "saints." Traditional "saintly" costumes could include early Christians such as Stephen, Paul, or Peter. Or for a unique twist, dress up as a Saint Bernard, a New Orleans Saints football player, or even St. Louis!

★ On the night of your All Saints' Eve celebration, have available costume-creating supplies for those who may need them. Some options include paper bags to create vests or shields, newspaper for hats, face paint, and dress-up clothes.

★ Steer clear of the traditional Halloween colors of orange and black. Instead, decorate the room with white sheets draped over chairs with polyester fiberfill placed on the floor and suspended from ceilings and doorways to create a peaceful, heavenly atmosphere. A few puffy pillow-clouds add to the atmosphere.

★ In addition to advertising your celebration within your own church, place an advertisement in the local newspaper or hang posters throughout your community advertising your alternative Halloween celebration. Simply enlarge and photocopy the poster on page 7. Parents of young children are always looking for safe, non-scary holiday activities.

★ Party prizes and festival favors could include small bags of cookies or other treats, colorful pencils, or tiny angel figurines.

FESTIVAL GAMES

Saints in Heaven

Simple Supplies: You'll need crayons or markers, blindfolds, masking tape, white polyester fiberfill, cloud-patterned gift wrap or a large piece of newsprint, and 3-inch white poster-board cloud shapes.

Directions: Before the festival, tape fiberfill "clouds" to a large sheet of gift wrap or newsprint, then tape the paper to the wall at a level all players can easily reach.

Give one or two white poster-board clouds to each player. Encourage families to talk about people they consider to be saints. These could be relatives or friends who are especially kind and loving. Tell families that we often call Christians believers or saints when they're caring, giving, and love to serve God and others. Encourage everyone to write the names of these people or draw their saintly faces on one side of the poster-board clouds. Have the families discuss what peaceful qualities these saints have that they would like to nurture in their own lives.

When everyone is finished, stand several feet from the paper on the wall. Hand each person pieces of tape to roll and to place on the backs of the clouds. Then play the game like Pin the Tail On the Donkey. Take turns blindfolding each other and trying to stick the poster-board clouds on or near the fiberfill clouds. Assure everyone that there are no right or wrong places to stick the saintly clouds. When everyone has had a turn to add the clouds to the wall, remind them that saints know, love, and follow Jesus—and that saints are loving kind people we can model ourselves after.

Peaceful Partnerships

Simple Supplies: No supplies required.

Directions: Explain that All Saints' Day, held on November 1, is a holiday to celebrate saints who have served God faithfully and promoted love and peacefulness among his people. These saints celebrated life on earth and the life we have in the Lord.

Congratulate families for choosing to celebrate life too. Then point out that this activity will demonstrate that peaceful partnerships, cooperation, and communication are ways to celebrate life.

Have family members stand in a circle and join hands. Instruct them to slowly lean in toward the center while keeping their legs straight and stiff. When everyone is leaning in, point out that each person is depending on his or her partnership with the entire circle to remain standing. Now encourage family members to work together to help the circle return to a standing position.

Put a fun twist on this activity by having everyone sit in a circle with backs scrunched in toward the middle so everyone's back is touching another player. Have families push cooperatively backward against each other until everyone is in a standing position. Can they return to sitting in the same way?

Invite families to tell about "peaceful partnerships" they have had and how being peaceable is important to living together happily. Remind everyone that God wants us to be peacemakers and to spread his love to others!

FESTIVAL CRAFTS

Angels Watchin' Over Me

Simple Supplies: You'll need scissors, white paper plates cut into eight wedges, pencils, Tacky craft glue, rolls of masking tape, and yellow construction paper. For each angel, you'll also need a flat 4-inch wooden spoon (available at craft stores) and a 1-inch length of self-adhesive magnetic strip. Be sure to provide enough supplies so each person can make an angel.

Directions: Tell families that the Bible reports God sending angels to protect people, to communicate his wishes, and to proclaim good news and great tidings. Explain that these lovely craft angels will remind them that peaceful angels watch over them each day.

For each angel, you'll need two paper-plate wedges. Trim the point off of each wedge. Then trace the milk cap on yellow paper and cut out the circle to make a halo. Trace around a roll of masking tape on yellow paper, cut out the circle, and cut it in half. These half-circles will be the angel's wings.

Glue the halo onto the large end of the spoon. If you'd like, draw a face on the angel. Then glue one paper wedge on the front of the spoon handle for the front of the angel's robe and the other wedge on as the back of the robe. Glue or tape the angel's yellow wings on the back of the robe. Peel the adhesive paper from the magnetic strip and stick it to the back of the angel's head.

As families make their Angel's Watchin' Over Me magnets, point out that many people believe angels are with them night and day. Read aloud Psalm 91:11, then briefly recount how the angel helped Peter escape from prison in Acts 12:3-18. Encourage families to visit about other stories in the Bible in which angels helped God's saints.

Saintly Silhouettes

Simple Supplies: You'll need large flashlights or bright desk lamps, several rolls of white shelf paper, tape, pencils, scissors, and markers. You'll also need a wall or door for people to stand against.

Directions: Have families create one-of-a-kind family portraits. Ask if families want their saintly costumes to be a part of their portraits. If not, they'll need to remove any hats or masks. Encourage families to work together.

Tape a 3-foot length of shelf paper to a wall or a door. Set the desk lamp on a table about 6 feet from the wall or hold a large flashlight so it shines brightly on the paper. Make the craft area as dark as possible, then aim the light so the shadows of each family's heads show up on the paper. The shadows can be increased or decreased in size by moving the light away from or closer to the family group. Then ask another family to trace the shadow's outline.

When the tracing is done, remove the paper from the wall and work together with the markers to add real or imagined details to each family member. You may wish to play soft music while families work.

Encourage family members to write the following Bible verse on the portrait: "To all . . . who are loved by God and called to be saints: Grace and peace to you" (Romans 1:7). These family portraits will be used later in the Festival Finale.

FESTIVAL FOOD

Heavenly Caramel Apples

Simple Supplies: You'll need several containers of frozen whipped topping, 12-ounce plastic cups, butterscotch-flavored instant pudding mix, several bags of apples, knives to cut the apples, and plastic spoons. You may wish to include dry roasted peanuts or miniature marshmallows.

Directions: Give each family one or two apples. Have an adult cut the apples into small bite-sized pieces. (No need to peel the apples.) Hand each person a plastic cup and spoon. Place 1 spoonful of butterscotch instant pudding mix into each cup, add 3 spoonfuls of frozen whipped topping, then stir the ingredients. Gently drop in several apple pieces and stir to coat them with the caramel topping. If you'd like, sprinkle your Heavenly Caramel Apples with dry roasted peanuts or miniature marshmallows.

While people enjoy these heavenly tasting treats, encourage them to visit about why they think heaven will be a peaceful place and how they can help earth be a more peaceful place today.

FESTIVAL FINALE

A Night of Peaceful Saints

Simple Supplies: You'll need a Bible and your Saintly Silhouettes.

Invite families to find quiet places to sit. Remind families that an angel helped Peter escape from prison. Read aloud the account from Acts 12:3-18. Ask families to name ways that Peter and the early Christians peacefully handled their crises. Then encourage families to think about and discuss one or more of these questions:

★ How did the angel help Peter peacefully resolve the crisis he was in?

★ What role do God and the saints mentioned earlier in the festival play in your everyday life decisions?

★ What steps can you take to guide others to peaceful alternatives within your family, your community, and the world?

Tell families that in the Bible, Christians who accepted Jesus as their Savior were called saints and that today when we know, love, and follow Jesus, we're often called believers or saints. Have families hold their Saintly Silhouettes and offer a prayer thanking God for being part of his kingdom and for the help of heavenly angels and the example of earthly saints who guide and help us live more peaceful lives. Then have family members sign their names on the portraits to show how proud they are to be saints in God's kingdom!

FAMILY FESTIVAL FOLLOW-UP

Peace-Filled Plan

Create a place in your home where you can go to peacefully settle disputes. Photocopy this list of suggestions and hand a copy to families as they leave. Tell them to post the list in the place they have designated as the Peace-Filled Corner.

★ Agree to solve the problem. Take turns talking. Tell the truth.

★ Tell the other family member how you feel about the problem.

★ Discuss how you could solve the problem.

★ Suggest ways to do things differently the next time.

★ Give each other a hug. Say, "I love you. God loves you!"

**Family
Faith Builder:**

Obedience

BOOK DAY

**Bring a book, take a look, and discover how
Josiah found the best book of all!**

BIBLE BASIS: 2 Kings 22:3-20

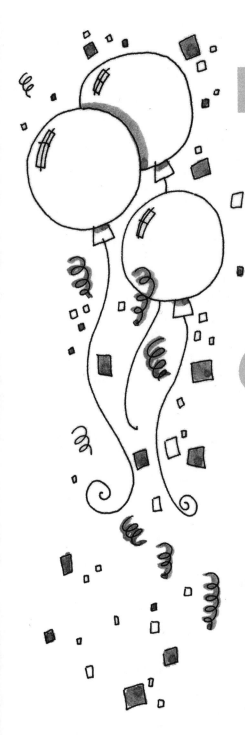

When was the last time you read a really good book? You
know the kind—you just can't put it down! When King
Josiah's secretary read to him from the Book of the Law
that had been found in the temple, Josiah knew this good book was
one that couldn't be put down—it must be obeyed. And through his
obedience, Josiah was saved from disaster. Become obedient to God,
grab his Book, and join other families on an afternoon in November
for games, goodies, crafts, and a "good read."

GETTING READY

Each activity in this family festival contains its own list of simple
supplies. Simply choose and use the activities that fit your needs
and time requirements, then gather the appropriate supplies. Use
one or more of these decorating and invitation suggestions to enliven your special event:

★ Create invitations on rectangular pieces of paper that can be
rolled up, scroll-like, and secured with ribbons. Use parchment
paper for a great touch!

★ Borrow books from your church library or bring some from
home to display throughout your festival room. Stand them up
with bookends or leave the pages open for families to browse
through during the festival.

★ Prior to Book Day, cut comic strips from the newspaper. Cut
the comic strips apart at the boxes and have families arrange each
comic in sequential order as they arrive for the event.

★ When advertising your festival, create a poster with unfamil-
iar words from the dictionary written on it as well as the information for your festival. Encourage all who pass by the poster to write

their own definitions for the words. At the Book Day celebration, read aloud their definitions along with the real definition and have families vote for the correct definition. What learning fun you'll have!

FESTIVAL GAMES

Josiah Says

Simple Supplies: You'll need a book for each person.

Directions: Have families play this game like Simon Says and experience a bit of obedience in the process.

Have each player choose a book to use during this game. Instruct everyone to find a place to stand and choose one person to be Josiah, the leader. Explain that this game is played like Simon Says, only the leader will ask players to do things with their books. Remind everyone to obey only if "Josiah says." If anyone performs an action without Josiah saying so, that player must balance a book on his head for three more commands, then rejoin the game. Have Josiah use commands such as, "Hold your books in the air," "Exchange books with someone else," or "Open and close your books." Change leaders after several commands and play until several people have had a chance to lead the group.

At the conclusion of the game, ask participants why they obeyed the commands. Have families discuss why being obedient is a choice we make and why it's important to choose to obey God.

Look, Look Scavenger Hunt

Simple Supplies: You'll need photocopies of the Look List from page 112, complete newspapers, and red markers or crayons.

Directions: Photocopy the Look List on page 112. You'll need one copy for each family group plus a few extras for visitors.

Explain to families that just as the carpenters, builders, and masons found the Book of the Law while working in the temple, they can hunt for and find newspaper treasures in this fun scavenger hunt.

To begin the game, hand each family a complete newspaper, a red marker, and a Look List. Encourage families to find all the items included on the Look List in their newspapers as quickly as they can. Highlight the located items in red.

When a family has found all the items on the Look List, have them shout, "We found what we were looking for!" You may want to award a recent issue of a national newspaper or a magazine such as *National Geographic* to the winning family. Remind everyone that books and written materials help us learn about our world, and the Bible helps us learn about God and ways we can obey him.

FESTIVAL CRAFTS

Temple Rubbings
Simple Supplies: You need plain white paper and crayons.

Directions: Point out that the Book of the Law (or Bible) was found in the temple by construction workers. In a similar way, families can get to know every square inch of your church with these Temple Rubbings.

Hand each person several sheets of paper and two or three colors of crayons. Encourage people to peel the paper off the crayons and to use the sides of the crayons for the rubbings. Turn families loose to go throughout the church making rubbings of different textures on their papers. To make a rubbing, place the paper over the texture you want to transfer, then rub the crayon back and forth over the paper until the texture appears. Remind participants to write what the rubbings were from on the backs of their papers.

When each person has filled her papers with rubbings, gather families and have them compare their treasures. See if people can guess or identify where each rubbing was made. Then attach your rubbings to a bulletin board for others to enjoy and examine in the coming weeks.

Scrolling Pillars
Simple Supplies: You'll need newspapers, scissors, and rubber bands or tape.

Directions: Tell families that they'll need to obediently follow the directions to make tall pillars that will remind them of the temple where Josiah's servants found the Bible.

Have each family open up a *sheet* of newspaper as if they were going to read it. Starting at the bottom, roll up the sheet until it's 2 to 3 inches from the top edge. Place another newspaper over the top edge of the first sheet, being sure the two papers overlap. Continue rolling the paper, stopping to add a third sheet of paper. Keep rolling and adding papers four more times. Roll the last piece of paper all the way up so that you have a long, skinny scroll, much as the Book of the Law may have looked when it was found.

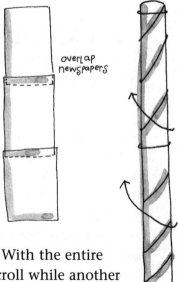

overlap newspapers

Holding the scroll carefully, make five 4-inch cuts into one end. With the entire family working together, have one person hold the bottom of the scroll while another puts his thumbs inside the scroll and gradually pulls the layers out. The pillar will become taller and taller. Keep pulling until it is 6 feet tall. Then hold the pillar and wrap rubber bands or tape around the base and sides.

Close by asking volunteers to briefly retell the story of how Josiah's workers found the Book of the Law when they cleaned and repaired the temple. Ask families how keeping the church looking neat and in good repair shows obedience to and respect for God.

FESTIVAL FOOD

Books-in-a-Bag

Simple Supplies: *You'll need large bowls of alphabet-shaped cereal, cereal loops, M&M's, pretzel sticks, raisins, sandwich-sized resealable plastic bags, and small paper cups.*

Directions: The book that the workers found in the temple didn't look anything like the books we read today. It was just a paper scroll, but it contained the most important words we could ever read—God's Word! Explain that these fun treats may not be good to read, but they're great to eat!

Set up a Books-in-a-Bag buffet line by placing the food items, paper cups, and plastic bags on a table. Invite participants to prepare their own treat mixes by using the small cups to dip individual food items into their bags. Have them seal and gently shake the bags to mix the ingredients.

Before anyone takes a bite of the crunchy mixture, have people use their mixes to obediently spell as many words from the Bible as possible. They can use the alphabet letters, the cereal loops for the letter "O," the M&M's for the letter "M," and pretzel sticks for the letters "L" or "I." See how many words each family can spell in 2 minutes, then invite them to enjoy munching the tasty treats.

Festival Finesse

As families munch their goodies, tell them that the Bible is by far the biggest selling book in history. Ask why they think that is, then encourage them to read from the Bible every day as a family.

FESTIVAL FINALE

Obeying God

Simple Supplies: *You'll need Bibles, paper, and pencils.*

Invite family groups to open their Bibles to 2 Kings 22:11-13 and to follow along as a volunteer reads the passage aloud. Then ask everyone to point out ways Josiah showed his obedience for God. Remind families that Josiah obeyed God because he had read God's Word and he knew it was the truth. Ask family groups to discuss one or more of these questions:

★ In what ways is obeying God easy? difficult?

★ Why is it important to obey God and his Word?

★ What is one way our family can show obedience to God this week?

Give each family a sheet of paper and a pencil. Encourage families to write down their answers to the last question, then take the papers home and put them in a prominent place to review—and to obey!—often during the coming week. Close with a prayer thanking God for the Bible and asking for his guidance as festival-goers try to be more obedient to him.

FAMILY FESTIVAL FOLLOW-UP

Book-It!

Organize a Book-It! collection drive for your church to collect book donations for a local library, women's shelter, nursing home, foreign missionary, or your own church library. Decide if you'll collect only Christian literature, children's books, or assorted types of books in all age levels. Decorate a large box and place it in a prominent area in your church. Encourage families to donate new or gently worn books. If books will go to your church library, provide labels so families can sign their names in dedication on the inside front covers. Distribute or mail the books to the appropriate agency.

Look List

Find the following items in a newspaper. Circle the items, then check the item off your list. Have fun!

❐ Find an ad selling a car for less than $2,000.

❐ Find your favorite comic strip.

❐ Find an article about a child or a family.

❐ Find a picture of a food item.

❐ Locate a picture of an animal.

❐ Locate a woman's name beginning with the letter "B."

❐ Find the weather forecast.

❐ Locate the date.

❐ Find a picture of clothing for sale.

❐ Find a television for sale.

HARVEST JUBILEE

Give glory and thanks to God during this fall festival.

BIBLE BASIS: Luke 17:11-19

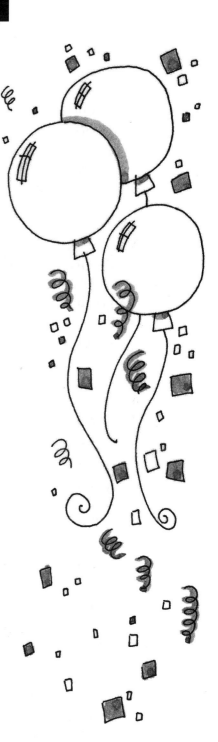

How many blessings do you have in your life? Do you have faith in God, a place to live, good health, a loving family? How many times have you remembered to say thank-you to God for all that he does for you every day? Just as the man with leprosy remembered to come back and thank Jesus for healing him, we can remember to thank God for all his blessings. This fall, on an afternoon or evening before Thanksgiving, gather families together to turn back to God and say, "Thank You!"

GETTING READY

Each activity in this family festival contains its own list of simple supplies. Simply choose and use the activities that fit your needs and time requirements, then gather the appropriate supplies. Use one or more of these decorating and invitation suggestions to enliven your special event:

★ Create invitations on thank-you cards. Enclose a beautiful autumn leaf in each envelope as an added seasonal touch. Give each family two invitations listing the time and location of your event. Then encourage families to pass on one of the invitations to another family within two days. See how many thankful families you'll attract to your event!

★ Surround yourselves with festive fall decorations, including pumpkins, shocks of grain, gourds, and lots of scattered leaves. A quick preservative for fragile fall leaves involves spraying fresh leaves with hair spray and letting them dry upside down. If you don't have fresh leaves available, encourage children in your congregation to tear out bushels of construction-paper leaves to spread on tables and floors and to hang on the doors and walls of your festival room. You can also use these leaves for the festival craft activity.

★ Festival favors and party prizes could include small baskets, shiny apples, silk leaves, and unusual gourds or squash.

FESTIVAL GAMES

Falling Apples

Simple Supplies: You'll need a paper leaf for each person, markers, tape, and two or three apples. (Use plastic apples if you'd like.)

Directions: Hand each person a paper leaf, then have players write their names on the leaves with markers. Tape the leaves on as name tags.

Remind families that they can be thankful God has given us loving families and so many good friends. Use this autumn game to get to know the names of others attending the Thanksgiving Jubilee.

Have families form two long lines facing each other. One player in the first line gently tosses an apple toward the second line and shouts, "I'm thankful for (name)." The player whose name is called tries to catch the apple as it is tossed. Then that player calls out, "I'm thankful for (name)!" and tosses the apple back to the first line. Keep gently tossing the apple back and forth as names are called. When everyone in both lines has been named, introduce another apple into the game to keep it lively.

Thank You, God!

Simple Supplies: No supplies required.

Directions: Ask families to shout out a few things they're thankful for. Then explain that this game will give them the opportunity to name many things for which they're thankful in many areas of their lives.

Have families sit in a large circle on the floor. Begin numbering off so that everyone in the circle has a sequential number. Begin the game by having participants start a rhythm by slowly slapping their legs twice, clapping their hands twice, and then snapping their fingers twice. Have players practice the rhythm until they are familiar with it. If some people have trouble snapping their fingers, tell them just to tap their fingers or to pretend they're snapping.

Begin the rhythm—slap, slap, clap, clap, snap, snap—then call out a number of someone in the circle while snapping your fingers. For example, your call might go: slap, slap, clap, clap, "Number 6!" Each time a player's number is called, he quickly names something to be thankful for. If this player "misses a beat" and can't come up with something, the entire circle stops the rhythm and shouts, "Thank you, God!" Then the person who missed a beat begins the rhythm again and calls another person's number. If the player called names something to be thankful for, the prior leader continues the rhythm and calls another person's number.

FESTIVAL CRAFTS

Paper-Bag Wreath

Simple Supplies: *You'll need brown paper grocery bags, scissors, narrow masking tape, 3/4-inch wide ribbon, construction paper, and preserved leaves or leaves torn from paper. Be sure you have two paper bags for each person.*

Directions: Ask families what autumn things we can thank God for. Then explain that this craft project will remind everyone of God's glorious autumn bounty.

Give each person two paper bags. (If you would like to make smaller wreaths, use lunch-sized paper sacks.)

For each wreath, begin by cutting the bottoms off of both paper bags, then cutting down one side of each bag to make two large pieces of brown paper. Place one bag on top of the other and roll them to make a long tube. Twist the bags slightly as you roll them together. Then tape the two ends together to form a circular wreath. Tie a ribbon bow over the tape to hide the ends of the bag. Tape preserved leaves around the wreath. If families use torn paper leaves to decorate their wreaths, encourage them to write on the leaves the names of people and things they're thankful for. Finally, add construction-paper berries or foliage to the wreaths. As families work, have them share about ways we can thank God for all he has given.

When the wreaths are complete, have families take them home to adorn their walls or hang on front doors as beautiful autumn decorations.

Thanksgiving Cornucopias

Simple Supplies: *You'll need ice-cream sugar cones, raisins, fruit-shaped cereal or fruit-shaped candies such as Runts, peanuts in the shell, candy corn or citrus slices, and tubes of decorating icing.*

Directions: This cornucopia table-favor can be used to decorate your Harvest Jubilee and then taken home to be used for edible name cards at Thanksgiving dinner.

Hand each person an ice-cream cone. Invite participants to use the tubes of decorating icing to write their names on one side of their sugar cones and then squeeze a small amount of icing on the inside bottoms of the cones. Fill the cones with a cornucopia of goodies such as fruit-shaped cereal, fruit-shaped candies, peanuts, raisins, or other treats.

As families are creating their Thanksgiving Cornucopias, encourage them to thank

God for all the good food he provides in the autumn. Invite each person to name his favorite Thanksgiving food. When the craft projects are finished, have families take them home to set on their Thanksgiving tables as lovely centerpieces.

FESTIVAL FOOD

Apple Kudos Dip

Simple Supplies: *You'll need apple wedges, chunky peanut butter, crispy rice cereal, miniature chocolate chips or raisins, a mixing spoon, measuring cups, and cereal-sized bowls.*

Directions: Explain that kudos are cheers we give other people to show we're thankful for them. Remind families that while they enjoy their Apple Kudos Dip, they can express why they are thankful for each member of the family.

Each family can make its own Apple Kudos Dip by measuring 2/3 cup of peanut butter and 1/8 cup of miniature chocolate chips or raisins into a cereal bowl. Stir the ingredients until the peanut butter is softened. Then sprinkle 1/4 cup of crispy rice cereal into the peanut butter mixture and gently stir the ingredients together. Distribute apple wedges to dip into the Apple Kudos Dip or provide a knife and clean apples to each family and let them slice their own.

Offer a prayer of thanks before "diggin' in," then encourage family groups to give each family member special kudos by telling reasons they are thankful for that person.

FESTIVAL FINALE

We Give Thanks, O God.

Simple Supplies: *You'll need Bibles.*

Have families open their Bibles to Luke 17:11-19 and follow along as a volunteer reads the passage aloud. Ask families why it's important to thank God for his blessings. Then challenge family groups to discuss one or more of these questions:
★ Who is one family member who could use your thanks right now?
★ How does being thankful affect our entire life?
★ What are ways we can express our thanks to God?
Encourage families to close with the following responsive prayer, thanking God for his constant love and care.

Leader: **For giving both the sun and rain,** Response: **We give you thanks, O God.**
Leader: **For always being ever the same,** Response: **We give you thanks, O God.**
Leader: **For sending your only dear Son,** Response: **We give you thanks, O God.**
Leader: **To love us, each and every one.** Response: **We give you thanks, O God.**
All: **Amen.**

FAMILY FESTIVAL FOLLOW-UP

Surprise Thanks

Remembering to say thank-you or to write thank-you notes after Christmas or your birthday is an expected part of any major holiday. But when was the last time you wrote a thank-you note to a Sunday school teacher you had long ago who had a lasting impact on you? Or what about writing a surprise thank-you note to a close friend who always is there when you need someone to talk to? Young children can become involved in this family activity by drawing pictures or dictating the notes to an adult to write. This meaningful act of kindness is a perfect family activity for a blustery autumn afternoon—while drinking hot cocoa, of course!

ADVENT NIGHT

Slow down the hectic holiday pace and focus on what Christmas is really about.

BIBLE BASIS: Luke 2:4-20

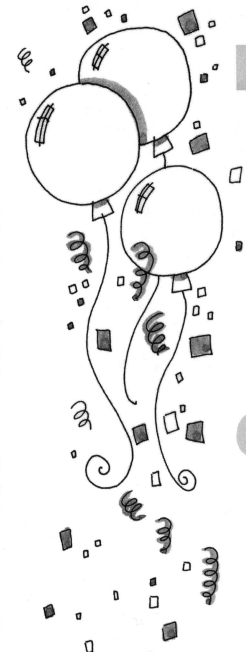

Many churches celebrate the season of Advent, which falls during the four weeks between Thanksgiving and Christmas. Advent literally means "the coming" and is celebrated as a reminder to prepare for the coming of our Savior, Jesus Christ. In the midst of hectic holiday hustle-bustle, many families often forget what the Christmas season is really about. Advent Night is an evening festival that allows families to reflect on the joy of Jesus' birth. Activities include Bible readings, holiday games, festive crafts, and a service project that helps others around the world prepare for and share in the joy of loving Jesus. Gather for this festive holiday happening during the first week of Advent to prepare families' hearts and minds for the coming celebration of Jesus' birth!

GETTING READY

Each activity in this family festival contains its own list of simple supplies. Simply choose and use the activities that fit your needs and time requirements, then gather the appropriate supplies. Use one or more of these decorating and invitation suggestions to enliven your special event:

★ String festive Christmas lights around the area to remind others that Jesus came as the light of the world.

★ Make small Advent wreaths to adorn tables. Use hot glue to attach three purple candles and one pink candle to an evergreen wreath. When your festival is over, have a drawing for families to take the wreaths home. Light one purple candle during each week of Advent and the pink candle on the Sunday before Christmas.

★ Hang crepe-paper streamers and balloons around the room, but instead of the traditional red and green of Christmas, consider using the colors of Advent, which include purple, pink, and white. Explain that purple is the color of royalty, promise, and preparation; pink represents love and joy; and white symbolizes Jesus' purity.

★ Cut out purple and pink construction-paper candles to use as invitations to the Advent Night festival. If your group of families is small, consider attaching colorful invitation notes to real candles.

FESTIVAL GAMES

The Road to Bethlehem

Simple Supplies: You'll need a Bible and a roll of crepe paper for each family or small group.

Directions: Be sure each family has a Bible. Tell families that this is a game of being prepared and that they must first prepare pretend roads to Bethlehem. Hand each family group a roll of crepe paper to unroll into a winding road. Roads may travel as far as your area permits, crossing other roads and winding around tables and hallways. Have all the roads end up at one place, such as the snack table or a particular door. Leave any unused portions of crepe paper at the end of the road.

Have each family group choose one person to be swaddled with crepe paper, one or more persons to be the wrappers, and the rest of the family members to be readers. Explain that you'll be reading aloud the story from Luke 2:4-20 of how Mary and Joseph traveled to Bethlehem to prepare for Jesus' birth. As readers retell the story, their families walk slowly along the paper roads.

As the story unfolds, have the wrappers carefully wind the crepe paper around the family member being swaddled. After you reach the end of the road, allow other families to guess who has been swaddled. Then carefully unwrap the swaddling bundles as families tell ways they can prepare for Jesus in their hearts and lives, such as through reading the Bible, praying, or being kind to others. Finally, have each family member tell one way she can prepare for Jesus in the coming week.

Prepare Through Prayer!

Simple Supplies: You'll need markers, plastic sandwich bags, and a roll of crepe paper for each family group.

Directions: Hand each family group a roll of crepe paper and several markers. Explain that this game is a brainstorm relay race and that the papers families prepare will be used in a craft project later. Mention that Advent is a time for preparation, promise, and prayer. Ask families to tell how prayer is a way that helps us prepare for Jesus and celebrate the promise of his love. Then have each family choose one person to be the slipster, one or more to be writers, and one or more to be tie-guys.

Have the slipsters tear off twenty-four 6-inch pieces of crepe paper while other family members brainstorm prayer needs. For example, prayer requests might focus on holiday travelers, families, sick friends, or world peace. Then have the writers write these needs on the slips of crepe paper. When each prayer need is written, have the tie-guys carefully tie the slips into half-knots. When families finish, have them jump up and shout, "Prepare through prayer!"

Have each family group place its twenty-four love knots in a plastic sandwich bag to use during the Prayer and a Kiss Calendars craft project. If you choose not to do this craft, send the bags home with the families at the end of the festival.

FESTIVAL CRAFTS

Prayer and a Kiss Calendars

Simple Supplies: For each calendar you'll need a 6-foot-long section of plastic wrap, scissors, twenty-four chocolate kiss candies or other wrapped candies, and twenty-four pieces of curling ribbon cut into 8- to 10-inch lengths. Decide before your festival whether to have each family or each person make one calendar, then purchase supplies accordingly.

Directions: Have family members help each other prepare these unusual Advent calendars. For each calendar, unroll a 6-foot section of plastic wrap on the floor. Evenly space twenty-four wrapped candies down the center of the plastic. Gently fold each side of the plastic in toward the candies. Then slide a piece of ribbon between each candy and tie it in a bow or knot. If you made the love knot prayer slips from "Prepare Through Prayer," tape them at random between the candies. When the calendar is complete, it will have twenty-four sections—one for each of the twenty-four days before Christmas.

On the first day of December, families should begin at one end of the calendar and snip off a candy section each day until Christmas. Each time a love knot is reached, open it and pray for the need expressed. Tell people that their Prayer and a Kiss Advent Calendars will remind them to pray for others as they prepare for Christmas. Remind everyone that God answered our prayers by sending his sweet Son, Jesus, to love us!

Awesome Angel Ornaments

Simple Supplies: For each ornament you'll need a 4-inch piece of white crepe paper, a 1-inch wooden bead, Tacky craft glue, pencils, fine-tipped permanent markers, and a 4-inch piece of thin gold wire or gold chenille wire.

Directions: These clever angel ornaments will remind everyone how God's angels helped the shepherds prepare to honor Jesus. For each angel ornament, squeeze a small amount of Tacky craft glue into the hole of a wooden bead. The bead will become the angel's head. Use a pencil to gently poke about half of the crepe paper into the hole of the bead to make the angel's robe. To make the angel's halo (and also the hanger for the ornament), make a loop with the gold wire, then gently poke both ends of the wire into the other end of the bead. You may need to squeeze in a small drop of Tacky glue to secure the halo in place. Use a fine-tipped marker to carefully add facial features. When the angel ornaments are dry, take them home to hang from family Christmas trees or use them to decorate the tree at your church.

FESTIVAL FOOD

Angel Food Sundaes

Simple Supplies: You'll need one or more angel food cakes, whipped dessert topping, and assorted toppings such as chocolate chips, crushed candy canes, crushed pineapple, chocolate syrup, chopped nuts, or candy sprinkles. You'll also need festive paper plates, napkins, forks, and spoons.

Directions: Set up your own Angel Food Sundae dessert bar. Invite people to prepare their own Angel Food Sundaes or have family members prepare sundaes for each other. For each sundae, top a slice of angel food cake with a dollop of whipped topping. Then have some fun by decorating the sundaes with any combination of colorful, flavorful toppings. As the special treats are nibbled, encourage people to visit about their family's special Christmas traditions. Tell why the tradition is a favorite and how it may help prepare them for the joy of loving Jesus. To make cleanup a snap, provide a wastebasket near the eating area.

FESTIVAL FINALE

Prepare Your Priorities!

Simple Supplies: You'll need Bibles.

Encourage family groups to find a quiet place to sit together. Have families open their Bibles to Luke 2:4-20 and follow along as a volunteer reads the passage aloud. Then ask everyone to point out ways God prepared Mary, Joseph, the angels, and the shepherds for Jesus' birth. Invite family groups to think about and discuss one or more of these questions:

★ How does your family prepare for Christmas each year? Which of these preparations focus on Jesus and the real meaning of Christmas?

★ Which Christmas preparations could you do without to leave more time to focus on preparing for Jesus?

★ How does preparing our hearts and lives for Jesus show him our love?

★ How can we help others prepare to love Jesus at Christmastime?

Encourage families to make a list at home of traditional Christmas preparations they'd like to continue and ones that center around preparing for Jesus. Then close with a prayer thanking God for his promise of Jesus and for the time we can prepare our hearts and lives to love him.

FAMILY FESTIVAL FOLLOW-UP

FAMILY FESTIVAL FOLLOW-UP

Operation Christmas Child

Operation Christmas Child is sponsored by the Samaritan's Purse, a Christian organization dedicated to bringing the joy of Jesus to children, especially at Christmastime. Each year, Operation Christmas Child sends over a million gift-filled shoe boxes to children around the world who may not know Jesus or have ever received a Christmas present. Church groups, families, and individuals fill shoe boxes with small gifts such as toys, personal grooming items, books, paper and crayons, small clothing items, and even letters or pictures for the children to keep. A $5 fee to pay for shipping must accompany each box sent to Samaritan's Purse. To receive a free Operation Christmas Child information kit and video, write or call:

Samaritan's Purse
801 Bamboo Road, P.O. Box 3000
Boone, NC 28607

PRESENTING JESUS!

Hold this exciting festival shortly after Christmas to celebrate the gift of Jesus.

BIBLE BASIS: Luke 2:25-33

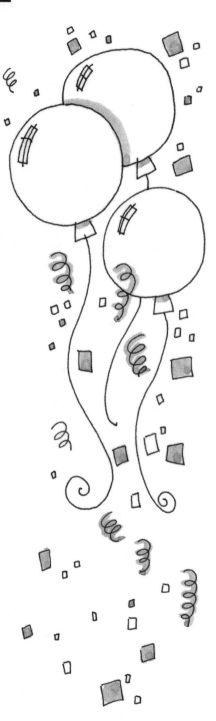

Gift-giving is such a predominant part of the Christmas season. We give gifts to family members, newspaper carriers—even our pets! But when does gift-giving become excessive and the gift of Jesus' birth overlooked? This year, after all the presents have been opened, stop and celebrate the season by focusing on the divine gift of Jesus. For an unusual twist, hold this festival in the middle of July to remind families that Jesus is God's special gift to us all year long!

GETTING READY

Each activity in this family festival contains its own list of simple supplies. Simply choose and use the activities that fit your needs and time requirements, then gather the appropriate supplies. Use one or more of these decorating and invitation suggestions to enliven your special event:

★ Make invitations by gluing photocopies of the festival information to squares of festive gift wrap, then rolling the invitations into scrolls. Tie them with a cascade of curled ribbons.

★ Decorate your festival room with beautifully wrapped gift boxes. You may even want to wrap the party tables and place large bows in the center of each table. Remember, hanging Christmas lights around the room gives it a festive glow!

★ Encourage families to bring old Christmas cards. These will be used for the Family Festival Follow-Up activity.

★ Advertise your event in the local newspaper or on the radio. The week of and following Christmas can be a lonely time for many people.

Hidden Gifts

Simple Supplies: *You'll need very small boxes (jewelry boxes work well), self-adhesive bows, and Christmas stickers with pictures of Jesus on them.*

Directions: Remind families that God sent his Son, Jesus, as a gift to the world. Point out that it's sometimes easy to forget or lose sight of this precious gift at Christmas when we get so caught up in receiving our own gifts from others. Explain that this game will remind them that Jesus is the reason for the season.

Have families form groups of eight to twelve people, then have them sit in a circle. Hand each group a small box, several stickers with pictures of Jesus on them, and a bow. Instruct players to place the stickers in the box, then add the bow to the top. Choose one person in each group to be the hider. Explain that the hiders will hide the groups' boxes around the room while everyone keeps their eyes closed.

When the hider returns to the group, have group members open their eyes and then take turns guessing where the box is hidden. The hiders will respond with "too far from Jesus" if a guess is far away from the hidden gift or "You're getting closer to Jesus!" if a guess is close to the hidden gift. Continue around the circle until the exact location is revealed. Then have the person who guessed correctly retrieve the gift, open it, and take out a sticker of Jesus to wear on his clothing. Then hide the gift again.

When the game is over, challenge families to discuss ways we lose sight of the true meaning of Christmas. Remind everyone that Jesus is the reason for the season and that we don't want to lose sight of our most precious gift!

Presenting Jesus Relay

Simple Supplies: *You'll need a Bible, baby blankets, baby dolls, small containers of baby powder, small bottles of baby lotion, and damp paper towels. If you can't find baby powder or lotion, use flour and a bit of milk.*

Directions: Explain to families that when Jesus was just a baby, he was presented to Simeon at the temple. Simeon had been waiting for the Savior his entire life, so when he held Jesus, he praised God and called Jesus a light to the Gentiles and glory to all God's people. Tell families that this relay race will remind them of how Jesus was presented to the world, to Simeon, and to us.

Have each family choose one person to be Simeon and to stand on the opposite side of the room—in the "temple." The other family members will stand in line and prepare the pretend babies for a trip to the temple. Hand families one each of these items in the following order: a doll and damp paper towel, baby powder, baby lotion, and a baby blanket. Explain that at the starting signal, each player holding a doll must give it a quick bath with damp paper towels, then gently pass the baby to the powder person, then to the lotion person, and finally, to the blanket person, who will wrap the baby in the blanket and run to Simeon. When Simeon holds the baby, he is to say, "A light for the world! Thank you, God!" The first family to get their sweet, clean baby to the temple wins. If there's time, play again but switch roles. Then gather everyone and read aloud Luke 2:28-32. Encourage families to discuss ways they can present Jesus to other people and ways they can praise God for the gift of Jesus.

FESTIVAL CRAFTS

Baby Jesus Ornaments

Simple Supplies: You'll need egg-carton cups, unshelled peanuts, gold metallic pipe cleaners, crimped paper stuffing (available in a bag by the gift wrap) or Spanish moss, scissors, Tacky craft glue, and markers.

Directions: Before the festival, cut the cups from egg cartons. Trim the edges to make them look neat. Prepare one cup for each person.

Remind families that Jesus' birth was special and holy, even though it took place in a barn. To be reminded of God's special and holy gift to us, nestle these ornaments on a branch of your Christmas tree or, better yet, leave them out all year.

Hand each person an unshelled peanut, a small clump of paper crimps or Spanish moss, an egg-carton cup, and a 3-inch section of gold metallic pipe cleaner. To make each ornament, wrap the gold pipe cleaner around the head of the peanut. Squeeze some glue on the inside bottom of the egg carton cup manger, then place the paper crimps or moss inside the cup to resemble hay in the manger. Place the baby Jesus peanut loosely in the hay. While families are assembling their ornaments, have them talk about ways Jesus was and is holy, humble, and honored by people who love him.

Be sure participants' initials are on the bottoms of the ornaments, then set them aside to dry before taking home.

Holy Gift Magnets

Simple Supplies: You'll need 4-inch squares of 1/2-inch-thick wood or Styrofoam, wrapping paper, scissors, tape, small gift bows, adhesive-backed magnetic strips, and photocopies of the Holy Gift poem at the end of this craft activity.

Directions: Distribute to each person a piece of wood or Styrofoam, an 8-inch square of wrapping paper, a 2-inch length of adhesive-backed magnetic strip, a small stick-on bow, and a photocopy of the Holy Gift poem. Wrap the wood in gift paper and trim away excess paper. Tape the top edge of the poem to the lower back of each present so the words hang down below the front. Stick the magnetic strip on the back center of each gift. Finally, place bows on top of the presents.

Have families work together to create Holy Gift Magnets for each person in the family.

Or suggest that families keep one and give the others to family and friends to whom they'd like to present Jesus.

HOLY GIFT

This is a very special gift
That you can never see.
It's like the special gift of Jesus
That God gave to you and me.

So leave it as you find it—
Don't even peek inside.
God's gift of love for you
Is one you cannot hide!

FESTIVAL FOOD

Crunchy Christmas Candles

Simple Supplies: You'll need long celery stalks, peanut butter, plastic knives, string licorice, and small paper plates.

Directions: Remind families that Simeon called Jesus a special light to the world. These edible treats will remind everyone that Jesus' light shines all year long and not just at Christmastime.

Have each family choose several celery stalks. Use plastic knives to cut the celery in 3- to 4-inch lengths. Give two pieces of celery to each person. Spread peanut butter inside the celery pieces, then lay a 4-inch piece of string licorice on one of the peanut butter halves so that it sticks up like the wick of a candle. Push the two celery halves together to create your very own Crunchy Christmas Candle. Hold the candles on small paper plates as if they were birthday candles on a birthday cake. Then invite all families to join in singing "Happy Birthday" to Jesus!

As families munch their candles, encourage them to discuss ways they think the gift of Jesus has changed the world and people's hearts.

FESTIVAL FINALE

Recycled Gifts

Simple Supplies: *You'll need Bibles, old (recycled) Christmas cards, and pencils.*

Invite family groups to open their Bibles to Luke 2:25-33 and follow along as a volunteer reads the passage aloud. Then ask people to point out ways Jesus' holiness was experienced by others in this passage. Challenge family groups to answer these questions:

★ How can God's gift of Jesus be remembered in your lives throughout the entire year?

★ In what ways can our family present Jesus to others who may not know him?

★ How can our family thank God for his most precious gift?

★ How can we put all of God's gifts to work in our lives?

Distribute the recycled cards and pencils. Have everyone write on the back of the card one God-given gift he or she could give to someone else. These gifts could include cooking dinner for Mom, vacuuming the living room, helping with homework, reading a book to a little sister, or helping clean the garage. Give the gift of these recycled cards to family members who would benefit from them. Close with a prayer thanking God for the gifts he has given each of us and for his loving gift of Jesus. As you say "amen," have families give each other loving hugs.

FAMILY FESTIVAL FOLLOW-UP

St. Jude's Ranch for Children

St. Jude's Ranch, home to more than fifty abused or abandoned kids, could use the gift of your family's recycled Christmas cards. Send your cards to St. Jude's Ranch, where the children create new cards to be sold at the ranch bookstore. Proceeds are given directly back to the kids to be used as spending money. Send your recycled cards to:

St. Jude's Ranch for Children
Box 60100
Boulder City, NV 809006